*"Imprisonment in a house or in a
palace is the same because
in both places is the desire of getting free.
To find complete freedom I have to go beyond desires.
I want to dive and dissolve in the ocean of peace."*

—St. Jhabban

Sweeper to

Illustrations by Elizabeth Ann Kelley

BABA HARI DASS

Saint

Sri Rama Publishing

©*1980 by Sri Rama Publishing*
P.O. Box 2550, Santa Cruz, California 95063
Sri Rama Publishing is a function of
Sri Rama Foundation, Inc., a non-profit organization
founded to produce the writings of Baba Hari Dass.
Profits from the books will go to support
orphans in India or the United States.
All rights reserved including the right
of reproduction in whole or
in part in any form.

•

Edited by Ma Renu
Typeset by Karunā Kristine Ault
Design, calligraphy, & display typography
by Josh Gitomer

•

First printing, September 1980
Second printing, December 1981
ISBN 0-918100-03-8
Library of Congress Catalog No. 80-52021

•

Cover photograph of a sunset on
the River Ganga (Ganges) at Rishikesh,
north of Haridwar, by Ma Renu.

•

The cover drawing of a sacred bull
is borrowed from the ancient tradition
of Sanjhi, a nearly extinct Indian
papercut folk-craft.

CONTENTS

Sweeper to Saint—10
Malang Sahib—70
Blind Poet—80
Destiny—94
Spiritual Wealth—124
True Master—142
Cave of Enlightenment—156

Sweeper to Saint

JHABBAN WAS BORN into a sweeper family in a small hill-town called Ranikhet. Sweepers are untouchables. Sweeping is their hereditary occupation. Even though sweepers are untouchables, they have always been an important part of the society in India. Without them there would be no cleanliness in the streets. If they stopped working, the garbage would pile up everywhere and the latrines would start flooding. That is why sweepers are called Mahattar, which in Sanskrit is the superlative degree of the word "mahat," meaning great. In fact they are the greatest, because without their help, the town, city or village would become a hell. Due to their hard labor, people were living in a heaven.

Jhabban inherited the rights to clean a street in Ranikhet, which was the largest street in the town. Before Jhabban, his father used to do the same work; but he had died from paralysis when Jhabban was ten years old. From six years of age, Jhabban used to help his father sweeping, so when his father died, he did not have much difficulty understanding his job, and he took on the full responsibility. He had a beautiful sister one year younger than himself, and his father, before he died, had married her to a young boy of another sweeper family working in the next street. Jhabban's father gave to his daughter as a dowry the sweeping rights of two houses which were connected to the street of the sweeper family into which she married.

Jhabban would work for the whole day. Every house paid him a fixed amount every month and gave him left-over food every day. Sometimes he would get old clothes, broken umbrellas, empty cans, etc. He had so much food that it was enough for ten people, but Jhabban had only his mother to care for. His sister had left for her husband's house and was working there as a part of that family.

Jhabban's mother started breeding pigs and she fed them the extra food which Jhabban would bring. The pigs were a great help in cleaning. Early in the morning Jhabban's mother would release them from the pigpen and they would eat all kinds of garbage thrown in the streets, which meant less sweeping for Jhabban. Sometimes, if the sewers were blocked, the pigs would go inside the sewers and pull out garbage blocking them. Her main purpose in breeding pigs was to sell them to meat suppliers to earn money. Jhabban saved his money from the people who paid him every month, and by selling pigs, the broken umbrellas, shoes and old clothes after repair, he came to be considered the richest among the sweeper community.

By the time Jhabban was thirteen years old, he had enough money to get married to a beautiful girl. Jhabban himself was not beautiful. He was short, fat, dark and round with a small potato nose and deep marks from smallpox on his face, which had also left him half blind in one eye. But he had money, so he was entitled to marry a beautiful girl from the sweeper community.

Every day Jhabban's mother received offers from different girls, and after finishing his work in the evening, Jhabban would dress in new clothes and go to the girls' houses. He wanted the most beautiful girl, so he rejected many girls. He was very proud of himself because he was getting so many offers. For him, marrying a girl was not so exciting as going to see a new girl every day. The parents of the girl would treat him as a prince.

Jhabban's mother was worried because her son had not accepted any girl yet. She was eager to see her son married as soon as possible; also, she wanted some help taking care of the pigs because they were increasing at a very fast rate.

At last Jhabban decided to accept someone. He went to see a girl living in the next town and he liked her. Jhabban got married, but after the wedding he was shocked to see that his bride was not the same girl he had chosen. This girl looked more or less like Jhabban. Also, Jhabban had been expecting that the girl's parents would give her much money, but they did not give her anything. Now he realized that he had been tricked by the girl's parents. The girl he had chosen was very beautiful and the girl he married was short, dark, fat and had deep marks from smallpox on her face, only her face was hidden by a veil. Jhabban and his bride looked like twins, but their natures were different. Jhabban was calm and cool minded; his wife, whose name was Jhumko, was a very talkative, hot-tempered person.

Sometimes Jhabban thought that he would not be able to stand living with Jhumko for very long. But he had to live with her because he believed that marriages are decided by God. Probably Jhumko had been his wife in several previous births. Jhabban's mother was also a very angry woman and would not tolerate any little mistake of Jhumko's. So the fight started as soon as Jhumko stepped into Jhabban's house.

Jhabban was still thirteen and so was Jhumko. For him marriage meant someone to take care of the pigs, cook the food, do the dishes, wash the clothes and treat him like a king. Jhumko knew all her duties because she had seen her brothers get married and how their wives had taken on that work automatically. But she took on the job of taking the pigs out and refused to do anything else. If her mother-in-law would ask her to do some cooking or cleaning, she would start cursing like a machine gun fired on the enemy.

Jhabban left his house very early in the morning and returned at noon. He would eat food and rest for an hour. Then he would go out again to his work and return when it was dark. He did not know about the fights between his mother and wife. Also, quarreling was not unusual in the sweeper neighborhood; fighting was a kind of emotional release for them. No one thought it was bad. It was like a custom.

But Jhumko was too much. She could not digest her food unless she cursed someone continuously for an hour. If there were no fights going on in the neighborhood, she would get very uncomfortable. She would take her dirty broom and throw it at someone's door, which meant a challenge. Sometimes, the fight would turn into physical violence, but only between the women. It would last only for a few minutes because some men would always come and separate them.

Jhabban spent the first seven years of marriage with Jhumko without really feeling that he had a wife. Then he began to feel that he needed a wife he could love. He tried to love Jhumko, but she only wanted to quarrel. Jhabban could not talk to her. When his mother, who was also famous in the neighborhood for quarreling, could not stand in the battlefield with Jhumko, how could Jhabban, who was very calm, stand in front of her?

WHEN A PERSON is unhappy in his family life, he seeks happiness somewhere outside. Jhabban started going to see his friends in the neighborhood. He had never really made friends with his neighbors before, because he had always been busy with his work. It was not difficult for the neighbors to understand why Jhabban was trying to be friendly now; they all stretched their arms open and accepted him. Jhabban was very happy to be with friends, and he felt very sorry for himself because he had lost seven years without enjoying the company of friends. He found that his friends were all very happy, but he was still not as happy as they were. One day he asked his friend, Khalifa, who was like the leader of all the young men, why he was not very happy yet. Khalifa at once said, "What kind of man are you? Did you ever take a puff of chandu?" (a smoke made of opium) Jhabban looked down and remained silent.

Khalifa pulled Jhabban by the hand and took him next door where all the men were sitting in a circle. In the middle, there was a small hole in the floor fitted with a long bamboo pipe. Khalifa at once made a place for Jhabban and himself in the circle. He took the pipe in his hand and chanted a few words. Someone put a burning twig over the hole and he took a deep breath, sucking the smoke into his stomach. Then he exhaled out the smoke into the mouth of the person sitting on his left. This one in turn swallowed the smoke and exhaled it into the mouth of the next person. In this way the smoke was swallowed by the whole circle. Jhabban was at the end of the circle, so he was the last one to swallow the smoke. He saw around the circle, how anyone who swallowed the smoke began to drop on the floor like a flying pigeon shot by a gun. When his turn came he was scared, but he did not want to be considered a coward, so he too swallowed the smoke and dropped on the floor in the same way as the others.

The next morning, they started moving their bodies and raising their heads up one by one like lizards. Some were still feeling drowsy, some had headaches and some left for their work. Jhabban felt great. He was very happy. His body was very light, energetic and refreshed. It was his first time and the chandu worked on him like a medicine. Now he understood why all his friends were so happy.

Khalifa was once a strong man in the community. Khalifa was not his real name, but people began calling him that, which means "leader" in Arabic, because he behaved like a leader in all activities. Now, due to his addiction to chandu, he could not work, and his wife and children had kicked him out of the house. He started a chandu business, and although there was no profit in this business, he could get chandu every day. Each person in the circle would bring chandu for one day and Khalifa would prepare the smoke.

For some time, Jhabban smoked the chandu of others and

then it was his turn to bring the chandu. He had enough money to buy it, so he bought chandu for everyone and they enjoyed it as usual. Jhabban was getting addicted.

Chandu creates a very strong addiction, which is almost impossible to break. The addiction creates much physical pain if a person can't get it. It also causes loss of memory, laziness and daydreaming. A chandu smoker can't work properly. It had happened to Khalifa and now it was happening to Jhabban.

Jhabban gradually began to make excuses for not doing his job. Sometimes his mother and sometimes Jhumko would work for him. He started selling the pigs secretly at cheap prices to buy chandu, and sometimes he would steal money from his mother's earthen pot buried under the ground.

All the women in the sweeper colony found out that the men were smoking chandu and they became very angry and blamed Khalifa for it. They all ran at him and beat him so badly that he left the community.

When Jhabban's mother found out that her hidden money had been stolen by someone and that the pigs were sold and that Jhabban was not going to work, she blamed Jhumko and Jhabban both. She at once sold all the remaining pigs and took over the work of sweeping the street by herself. She fed leftover food to Jhabban and Jhumko, considering them now to have taken the place of the pigs. For Jhabban it was okay, except that he wanted to have some money for buying chandu, but for Jhumko it was a great insult, and she told Jhabban that he should take her back to her parents. She said she was not going to live with him any more if they were treated like pigs.

Jhabban was very addicted to chandu; he was very depressed because he had not been able to smoke for two days. He decided that if he went to his father-in-law's house, they might give him some money, at least the expenses of bringing their daughter back, and with that money he could buy chandu. So he at once said, "Yes, I'll take you to your parents. Let us go."

They walked on foot for twelve miles. Jhabban knew the shortcut bridle path, otherwise it would have been twenty-seven miles. They arrived there in the evening and Jhumko's parents were very surprised to see her back. They thought that she must be pregnant and wanted to talk to her mother, but when they realized that she was not pregnant, but had left Jhabban, they became very angry at Jhabban. They were not angry because he was addicted to chandu, but because they were afraid of Jhumko's fighting; they wanted to stay away from her.

Jhabban was expecting to get some money from them and he had a plan all made in his mind about finding Khalifa, buying chandu and finding a place to fix the smoking pipe. Here he found out that they wanted him to take Jhumko back, which meant another great fight with his mother. He had no place to go. His street clients, which he inherited from his father, had disowned him and had given the job to his mother. Now he had no right to go there. If he had been single, then probably his mother would allow him to live in the house and would feed him in place of the pigs. But she would never allow Jhumko to live with her again. In her mind, Jhumko was the cause of all the disaster.

Jhumko's parents allowed Jhabban to stay overnight. They knew that Jhumko couldn't live anywhere because of her nature. They were very surprised that Jhabban had been able to live with her for seven years. Jhabban was given a few pieces of bread with salt to eat and they showed him a corner and a gunny sack where their dog, which had died a couple of days ago, used to sleep.

After he had eaten, Jhabban lay down on the gunny sacks. He was very uncomfortable due to not smoking chandu. All the time, the vision of smoking chandu would appear in his mind. His body was aching and the fleas on the gunny sacks, which had also been hungry for two days, started sucking his blood at once. Jhabban could not sleep at all and decided to leave for his house at midnight. He stood up and very secretly crept into the next room where Jhumko and her mother were sleeping. He had not come to this room to see Jhumko, but it was the only way to get out of the house. All of a sudden, a thought hit his mind, "Why don't you steal their ornaments? You can sell them and can get money to buy chandu."

Jhabban sat down and began to grope around with his hands on the dirt floor in the dark to see if he could find something—ornaments, clothes, shoes, anything. Once, his hand touched his mother-in-law's arm and she rolled on her side, snoring in deep sleep. Jhabban put his hand under her rug and found a handle sticking up. He pulled the handle up and a box, which was hidden under the rug and buried in the ground, came out. Jhabban took the box very quietly, and without delaying any more, left the house. In the dark, he could not see where to go, but he had to get away as soon as possible. So he started walking and found a footpath. He walked all night and in the morning, he found himself near a river. He was very tired so he sat down under a tree. He opened the box and found it was full of silver coins. He at once remembered that he had stolen his mother's money, which had been hidden in the same way. Now he was very happy because he had enough money to buy chandu for a month. But he was afraid to go home. Jhumko and his mother-in-law would surely go to his mother's house when they found out that the money had been stolen. Also, Jhabban did not know where he was. After resting for an hour, he took a path which was going straight to a mountain top.

While he was climbing, hungry and tired, he began to think how he had been so happy and free when he did his sweeping job all day and made money by selling pigs and old clothes. He was rich in the community, but as soon as he desired a wife, all sorts of troubles began to come. He started smoking chandu, he started stealing money and he stopped working. Another thought arose in his mind—that he should go back to his mother-in-law's house and return the box. But then again the addiction of chandu knocked on his head and he said to himself, "My mother-in-law also cheated me. She showed me a beautiful girl and then married Jhumko to me. If I steal the money of a cheat, then there is no sin. They deserve some punishment."

Jhabban's arguments supported his robbery of his mother-in-law, but the problem of where to go now was still standing in front of him like a demon in the form of a question mark.

For the first time, Jhabban felt afraid of people. He was almost on the top of a mountain when he came to a little village.

A few people were working on their corn fields. Jhabban was afraid they would ask, "Who are you? You seem like a thief." "Probably they will beat me," he thought. "Or if they find the box of money, they will snatch it." His mind began to worry about everything. If his hand would touch a bush as he walked by, he would get scared and imagine that someone was trying to catch him. He began to look around very suspiciously, yet he continued climbing the path and hiding behind the bushes.

A villager was passing stool behind a bush near the footpath and when Jhabban sneaked by the bush like a cat, the villager stood up, startled. Jhabban and the man were face to face with the bush in between. Jhabban was already very afraid and when he saw someone pop up in front of him right behind a bush, he screamed very loudly and dropped down on the ground in a faint.

The villager felt very guilty about this and called all the villagers who were working nearby. They decided to take Jhabban to their hut where he could rest and come back to his senses. They lifted Jhabban and brought him to their hut, where they put him on a wooden table over thick blankets. They put water on his head and in his mouth and sprinkled it over his face and chest. They unbuttoned his coat and shirt so that air would cool his chest. He was sweating and still unconscious. The villagers found the box tied to Jhabban's waist and pressing into his back, so they removed the box from his waist and placed it by his side.

Jhabban came back to his senses, but he had a fever. He was very weak and unable to stand up. He remained lying on the table. Suddenly he remembered about the box. He felt his waist and it was not there. He sat up with a jerk, his eyes wide open, and began to look at the villagers. He said, "Who took my box?" The villagers at once showed him the box by his side and Jhabban again dropped back on the table, clutching his box with both hands.

The fever began to increase and at night, Jhabban began to hallucinate. Sometimes he would scream with fear and sometimes talk to Khalifa about making chandu. The villagers did not understand anything. They were very sympathetic towards him. For two days, his fever and delirium continued, but on the third day his temperature was normal and he was quite sensible.

By now, he was completely confident that the villagers would not snatch his money, but he had another fear: if they found out that an untouchable sweeper had been staying in their house, they would never forgive him. Although he was very weak, he began to seek a chance to slip away from the village. The villagers were so impressed to see his simplicity that they wanted him to stay in the village forever.

Someone would sit in the hut all the time. Not because of Jhabban, but because of monkeys who would ruin everything in the house if they saw no one there. There were several dogs in the village to chase monkeys and they would run around in the fields barking all day long.

Jhabban stayed there for seven days and then he was strong enough to resume his journey, so he requested that the villagers permit him to leave. He did not tell where he was going because he himself did not know. He did ask where the footpath would take him. The villagers told him that at the bottom of the mountain there was a dense forest. The path led to the edge of the forest and reached the last railway station, named Kathgodam. From Kathgodam he could either go to Bareilly by train or go the Nainital or Ranikhet hill stations by bus.

After getting all this information, Jhabban left the village and happily started his journey to Kathgodam.

He was brought up in the mountains so it was easy for him to walk on mountain footpaths, up and down like a monkey; but when he reached the flat land where the sun was hot and the ground was burning, he felt uncomfortable. He could not walk very fast and stopped often to rest under the shade of trees.

It took him two days to reach Kathgodam. The villagers had given him food for the way, so he was not hungry or tired. In the meantime he began to forget about chandu, partly due to his sickness and partly due to walking all the time. Still, sometimes he would visualize the chandu smoking circle, but the desire to smoke chandu was not so intense as before.

Jhabban reached Kathgodam and without knowing anything about Bareilly, he bought a train ticket for that city. He only knew that Bareilly was a big industrial city and that getting a job there was easy, but he did not know that living there was full of danger. All kinds of bad people were working there in mills, factories and small cottage industries.

JHABBAN REACHED Bareilly and left the railway station. He thought he should see the city first and then look for a job. As he was walking towards the city, a man from a colony waved his hand to Jhabban asking him to come in. It was a compound of the New Christian Mission. When Jhabban got near, the man said, "At last, Peter, you came back. I knew you would surely come." Jhabban did not understand; he began to look around to see if someone named Peter was behind him to whom the gentleman was speaking.

The man said again, "Peter, what happened to you? Don't you remember me? I am Doctor Robert Hey." Jhabban began to put pressure on his mind to remember whether this man had been living in Ranikhet in the street where he used to sweep. If this were so, then he did not want to stay there for a moment. But he knew all the faces of his street. This man had never lived there and he had never met him before. Then Jhabban raised his head and said, "Sir, probably you are taking me for some other person named Peter. My name is Jhabban. I have never been in Bareilly before."

Dr. Hey said, "I can't believe it. Do you have a twin brother?" Jhabban said, "No, I have a younger sister but we don't have any similarity in our physical appearance and she also never came to Bareilly."

Dr. Hey said, "Peter lived with me for four years and only two months ago he left because he had some quarrel with my wife. I never wanted him to leave. He also did not want to leave that I knew, but he left anyway."

"Do you want a job?" Dr. Hey asked. Jhabban said, "Yes!" without asking what kind of job it was. Dr. Hey at once jumped up happily and said, "Dorothy, come here! Peter is back." Dorothy came out and said, "Peter, forgive me. It was my mistake, but I was trying to blame you. I knew you would come back. Now resume your job as usual." Jhabban remained standing perplexed. He did not know what his duty was.

Dr. Hey laughed loudly and said, "Dorothy, he is not Peter! Not even Peter's twin brother, maternal brother, relative or even from Peter's town."

Dorothy said, "I don't believe you. Don't fool me. You told him to act like a new man to make a joke. I know your tricks." In the meantime, the children came back from the school and they leaped on Jhabban saying, "Peter, when did you come? Why did you leave? We missed you so much."

Hearing the noise of laughing children, others from the mission camp collected and said, "Peter, you returned. You are a good boy."

Now Jhabban automatically turned into Peter. Everyone called him Peter. Most people never thought that he was not the same Peter.

Jhabban in Peter's place picked up his duties very fast. His walking, talking, body gestures, everything were exactly the same as Peter, but Dr. Hey noticed some difference. Jhabban was very smart whereas Peter was dumb. Both were very cool, kind and loving. Naturally, Dr. Hey's interest in the new Peter began to increase and instead of putting him in a house job, he put him in the hospital to work with him as a nurse.

Jhabban was not very interested in a house job, because there was no excitement in sweeping the floor, cleaning windows, tables, and so on. But he was very enthusiastic about working in the hospital, cleaning wounds, administering medicine and bandages, and slowly he learned how to inject medicine. Some people have some kind of healing power in their hands. Peter (Jhabban) had the same power. His touch was so gentle that it would delight the hearts of patients. There were several trained nurses and interns, but patients would prefer Peter to give them medicine or shots. Slowly, patients began to say that Peter was a doctor who could cure any patient, and they began to call him Dr. Peter.

It was well known in the hospital that if Peter cleaned a wound and put medicine on it, it started healing immediately. If he gave medicine, the fever began going down to normal immediately.

At first Dr. Hey did not understand why all the patients wanted Peter to give them medicine. Slowly he heard stories from patients that whoever got medicine from Peter was cured. He also heard patients calling him Dr. Peter. It made him very happy. He knew that Peter was very intelligent, but he had no faith that the medicine worked better if given by Peter. He thought it was a superstition spreading among the patients that Peter had healing power in his hands. He could accept that a person could be expert in surgery, because it is an act of hands and concentration. He would accept that Peter cleaned the wounds so gently that the patient never felt any pain. He saw it with his own eyes.

Now Dr. Hey encouraged Peter to concentrate more on his work. He began to take him into the operating room so that he would be well acquainted with different instruments. He also would take him to visit out-patients.

Month after month passed and Peter became famous. His experience was greater than that of a doctor who studies in a medical school. When he first came to the mission camp, he did not know how to read or write, but the name of every instrument in the hospital or any kind of medicine and its use was imprinted in his mind. He was so absorbed in his work that he completely forgot about chandu, his friends, mother and wife.

One day Dr. Hey was called by the prison officials to examine a patient who had an infection on his arm from a knife wound. Dr. Hey took the necessary medicine and instruments and went to the prison. He examined the patient and saw that it was really a serious wound. He told the prison official in charge that his assistant would come to the prison to clean the wound and dress it every alternate day, then he left for his hospital. Dr. Hey appointed Peter for the prison duty. One day while Peter was bandaging the wound of the patient, he heard someone calling from the other side of the cell, "Jhabban you are here." First he forgot that his name was Jhabban, but when he heard it again and again, he looked in the cell on the other side of the corridor. He saw Khalifa standing, holding the iron bars of the gate.

Peter at once said, "Khalifa, you are here? How did you come to this prison?" Khalifa said, "Oh, nothing. I stole a box of money from the neighborhood and they reported it to the police. The police arrested me and now I am here."

Peter at once recalled the chandu. For a moment his desire for chandu opened up. Then he remembered stealing his mother's hidden money; and he also remembered that he had stolen his mother-in-law's money box. His head began to swim. He at once said, "Khalifa, I will talk to you afterwards. I have to go to my work."

Peter reached home feeling very guilty about stealing his mother-in-law's money. He said to himself, "I was in need of money and I stole it, but now I have enough money. I can return hers. There were 35 silver coins in the box. Now I can send her four times more." He at once went to Dr. Hey and asked him to send 140 rupees to his mother-in-law. Dr. Hey, without asking any questions, filled out the money order form. On the bottom, Peter requested that he write this letter to his mother-in-law:

"Dear Gyano: I stole the 35 rupees which were hidden in a box under your bed. I am sending you 140 rupees. I hope you will forgive me for my wrong actions."

At first, Dr. Hey was very shocked that Peter had stolen money. "He is so calm. Why did he steal money?" he said to himself.

Peter noticed his thoughts and said, "Sir, it's true. I really stole money from my mother-in-law's house. I also stole my mother's money, but I am not a thief. At that time I wanted money and now I don't need money. It seems that you are afraid I'll steal money from your house, aren't you?" The doctor said, "Oh, no Peter, no. I was just wondering why you did that. I know you don't steal money."

Peter changed the subject and said, "Sir, there is one bedroom vacant in the hospital. If you permit, I'll sleep there, because I can give more time serving patients if I live in the hospital."

Dr. Hey actually was a little afraid that Peter might steal money from his house, so he at once said, "Yes, Peter, you can stay anywhere you want. You can get your food from the hospital kitchen. You are on the permanent staff of the hospital."

Peter had never asked for his wages and had never cared if he was the doctor's private servant or permanent staff of the hospital. All of his needs were fulfilled by Dr. Hey.

The New Christian Mission was a group of people who helped poor people in various ways. They had a hospital, a children's school, a church and a small vegetable garden. The main idea of the mission was to convert non-Christians into Christianity. In their belief, those who were Christians were entitled to salvation, so their purpose was to give salvation to non-Christians by converting them to Christianity.

Dr. Robert Hey was the originator of the New Christian Mission in Bareilly. He was a European Christian, probably from Germany. He was in his fifties and was very sincere in his work. He was not only a doctor, he was a Christian minister, too. He had the firm belief that as soon as a person was baptized into Christianity, all of his sins were gone and he attained salvation. His wife was equally devoted to serving people and converting them to Christianity.

When Jhabban came to this camp, he was from an untouchable Hindu caste, but he appeared there as Peter. The former Peter was Dr. Hey's servant and was converted to Christianity by the doctor. So considering Jhabban as Peter, no one had ever asked him about Christianity and no one imagined that he was not a Christian.

To Peter, Hindu, Moslem, Christian—all religions were the same. Untouchables would remain untouchable regardless of what religion they convert to. This was his belief. In spite of this, he would attend church every day just like the others; but for the others, going to church was part of the job and for Peter it was different. He would listen to every word of the priest and think about it. He enjoyed the prayer. He enjoyed the different stories, but when he was told that he should trap non-Christians for conversion, he felt uncomfortable. He thought, "If a person himself is honest and on a right path, then he doesn't need to say to others, 'Follow me, I'll take you to heaven.' People will automatically follow him."

After sending money to his mother-in-law, Peter felt much relief. He felt as if a great burden had been removed from his mind. The next day, he went again to the prison to see his patient. When he passed through the corridor, he saw Khalifa standing and holding the iron bars of the door. Probably he was waiting for Jhabban.

When Khalifa saw Jhabban passing, he yelled, "Jhabban, come here!" Jhabban turned toward Khalifa's cell and said, "Khalifa, no one knows me as Jhabban. My name is Peter. I am a Christian. I am no longer an untouchable Hindu sweeper." Khalifa did not know anything about Christianity. He only knew that he was from the untouchable class. His mind was all burned up from smoking chandu, so there was no space for thinking about the past or future. He was only concerned about the present. For him, if the present was okay, then everything was okay. For him the highest religion was that where he could get chandu. Any person who gave him chandu was more than God for him.

He said, "Jhabban, I don't understand what you are talking about. Don't you remember? I am Khalifa. I know you, you are Jhabban. We used to smoke chandu together, remember?"

Peter realized that it was useless to talk to Khalifa because he didn't understand anything. So he said, "Khalifa, you are right. I remember everything. Tell me, how do you get chandu here?" Khalifa looked around and said, "Everything is available here." Then he whispered something in Peter's ear. Peter looked at him sternly and said, "Sin, Khalifa, it is a sin. You get what you give. The prison guards and you are both sinners. I don't want to hear about it any more. My work here will be completed today and then I'll not visit the prison any more. I live at the mission hospital; in case you get sick and want to see me, let me know."

Khalifa said, "I am here for only two months more. Then my two years will be completed. I am happy here. I don't have to do anything all day. I only sleep. At night I am free. I can go anywhere I want. I won't be happy to be released. Do you know it is the best place for me."

Peter was late so he said, "Khalifa, goodbye. I have to work," and he left to see his patient. His patient was almost healed and no more medicine was necessary. He took off the bandage and told the patient to let the wound dry by itself. He left for the hospital. On the way, he thought that if Khalifa came to the mission camp when he was released, the doctor would surely give him a place to stay, because he wanted to convert as many non-Christians into Christianity as possible. He didn't know what kind of man Khalifa was. "Khalifa will bring blame on me with his bad habits. If I tell Dr. Hey not to allow Khalifa to stay in the camp, he will never listen and will start giving lectures on Christianity."

In the evening, Dr. Hey went to see the patients in the hospital. Peter followed him as usual. Today, he was not so cheerful as before, but Dr. Hey did not notice it. When Dr. Hey had visited all the patients, he told the patients that those who could walk should attend church. Most of the patients were very poor and had no means of livelihood when they were released from the hospital. Such patients were very easy to convert, because Dr. Hey would give them food, clothes, work and a place to stay. So the New Christian Mission in Bareilly was growing very fast.

When Dr. Hey was about to leave for his house, Peter said, "Sir, I want to leave for a few days. I think I must see my mother, relatives and neighbors."

Dr. Hey said, "Peter you can't go. Don't you understand that no one else can work in your place? All the patients need you. A true Christian should serve the poor. Look at me. I left my homeland when I was seventeen and never went back to see my parents." Peter realized that the doctor would not let him go, so he said, "Sir, a true Christian is he who brings people to Christianity." The doctor thought awhile and said, "Peter, you are also right. Maybe you can bring your whole family here. Yes, you can go, but return as soon as possible. Bring as many people as you can."

The next day Peter was not in the hospital. No one knew

where he had gone. The doctor also forgot about his talk with him and was worried. Then he remembered that Peter had gone to bring his whole family to Christianity.

Day after day passed. The work in the hospital was less smooth each day. Dr. Hey began to feel that everyone wanted him to say what to do. No one was taking interest in serving patients as Peter had.

Then one day Peter appeared, very mysteriously. He was wearing old rags; he had a long beard and moustache, and uncombed hair. The doctor at once recognized him and told him to take a bath, shave his beard and put on his clothes. Peter threw away his dirty sheath and came out clean as he had been before. Dr. Hey said, "Peter, without you, the hospital can't function very well. Everyone wants me to tell them what to do. I am getting tired from so much work. I am happy that you came back. Now take your job in the hospital."

Peter said, "Sir, I can't work in the hospital. I don't know anything about it. I can work as I was working before." The doctor said, "Yes, do the same work you were doing before in the hospital." Peter did not understand anything and started working in the doctor's house as before.

This was the real Peter, but no one could tell that he was not Jhabban. When the doctor saw him working in the house, he realized that he was the former Peter. His happiness dimmed because he knew this Peter was dumb and couldn't do anything except clean the house and sweep the floor. But the doctor knew that if he took this Peter with him to the hospital, the patients would feel that Peter had returned and they would be happy. He said to himself, "I know this Peter can't give them medicine, wash their wounds or give shots, but I can use him to make them happy."

So the real Peter would work in the house and would also go to the hospital with Dr. Hey, just like Jhabban. Everyone noticed some difference in the work of the former Peter and this Peter, but no one paid much attention to it. The work began to flow better in the hospital because of their faith in Peter (Jhabban).

Khalifa was released from the prison and he started roaming in Bareilly city, sometimes begging food and sometimes hauling bags from one place to another to earn money. After a few months of roaming like this by chance he saw Peter standing at the gate of the mission camp. He at once rushed to him and hugged him and said, "Jhabban, I found you. I found you. I forgot your address and name." Peter was very surprised to see an unknown person acting as if he was his dear friend.

He said, "Who is Jhabban? My name is Peter." Khalifa at once yelled, "Yes, Peter, Peter. I forgot. Now you are Peter. I'll call you Peter."

Peter took Khalifa to the doctor thinking him crazy. Also he knew that the doctor wanted people to come to the mission camp for help.

The doctor talked to Khalifa with much professional love and said, "Khalifa, you can stay in this camp if you are looking for a place. What kind of work can you do?"

Khalifa said that he could sweep the hospital and clean the sewers and latrines. The doctor needed a man who could do just this work, so Khalifa was appointed as a hospital staff member.

For Khalifa, Peter was his intimate friend, Jhabban. But he knew that he was not supposed to call him Jhabban, so he called him Peter just like the others. But in his heart he felt him to be Jhabban, his chandu smoking friend.

Peter was not very smart, but when he saw that someone loved him so much, he also started loving him equally. Whenever Khalifa would say something about some events of the past, he would get confused, but he did not pay much attention to it.

Khalifa got his monthly pay; it was not very much, because his food and clothes were free. He at once went to the market and bought all the stuff for chandu, because he knew his friend Peter would accompany him. If he had been alone, he would go to some chandu den. Smoking chandu alone is no fun.

At night Khalifa secretly went to the doctor's house and entered Peter's room. He asked Peter to come to his room and said he had a surprise for him. Peter was very excited to hear about the surprise and at once went with Khalifa. In the center of the room Khalifa had made a hole in the floor and fixed a pipe. He covered it with a cloth to make it a surprise. When Peter stood in the room, Khalifa removed the cloth saying, "Ta-Ta!"

Peter said, "What is this? Is it a chandu pipe?" Peter had seen people smoking chandu, but he had never smoked. Khalifa said, "Don't you remember? Oh, you don't remember anything. You are Peter now. I bought everything today from my month's pay. Now we can smoke chandu every day."

Peter wanted to experiment with chandu. He had heard so much about it from chandu smokers. He saw how people smoked it in a circle. It didn't take much skill to smoke chandu. So both friends sat face to face and Khalifa held the pipe and asked Peter to light a match on the top of the hole. There was very little chandu stuff because they were only two people. Khalifa sucked the smoke and then they passed the puff in each other's mouth two or three times. They both dropped on the ground motionless.

In the morning, Peter opened his eyes and found himself in Khalifa's room. He at once stood up and left for his room. Khalifa was still out of his senses, because he had taken two puffs more than Peter.

Peter felt very good. He felt much energy in his body. He was happy. He said to himself, "Really, chandu is something. That's why chandu smokers praise it so much."

Khalifa's duty was from 10 a.m. to noon so he was not worried about his work, even after coming to his senses. For him, chandu was his life. Without smoking chandu, he would get very stiff, as if his joints were made of wood. Also, he could not work.

In the evening, Khalifa prepared chandu and waited for Peter to come. He knew Peter would come by himself and he did not go to call him. Peter had finished his house duty and he went to Khalifa's room. He was trying to forget about smoking chandu, but when he went to his room, instead of changing his clothes, he straightened his bed, closed the window and then, unknowingly, his feet began to walk towards Khalifa's house as if Khalifa were pulling him with hypnotic powers.

When Peter entered the room, Khalifa said, "I knew you would come, Peter. It is no fun to smoke chandu when there are only two. Why don't you bring the gardener and cook here? They are your friends. I am a new man here. I can't talk to them." Peter said, "I talked to them about chandu and they were very excited about it. They want to try it. They can't come until nine o'clock. Let us go for a walk and when we return, we will bring them from the kitchen." Khalifa agreed to Peter's idea. They went out to the road and headed towards the city. Khalifa's mind was on chandu. He did not want to be late or forget to come home. They walked about a mile and Khalifa said, "It's late. Let us go back." Peter did not want to return so soon. There was still one hour to wait for the cook. He crossed a street and said, "Khalifa, we will go back through the other end of town." They crossed a few streets and in one street there was an opium dealer living in a corner. The opium dealer was an old, thin man sitting on his cot outside of the house near the street. When Khalifa and Peter passed him, the old man said, "Khalifa, how are you?" Khalifa at once recognized the man. They had met a few times in a chandu den, and in the circle they had sat side by side. Khalifa stopped and said, "Ajmal, do you live here? I remember, I came here to smoke chandu." The old man, whose name was Ajmal, whispered, "That den belongs to me and I am an opium dealer. I have a license from the government to sell opium. My opium business is inside my house. My customers know about it, so I don't put up any sign to make it look like a store."

Khalifa tried to see inside the house from the street but it was dark inside, and only a thin candle was burning on a table. The talk about chandu, opium and smoking with Ajmal excited Khalifa's desire to smoke so much that he could not wait any longer. He said, "Peter, let's go now," and started walking very fast. Peter followed him.

As soon as Khalifa and Peter moved out of sight of Ajmal, a man came out of Ajmal's house and disappeared very secretly into a dark street, like a cat. The man did not want to be seen by Khalifa and Peter. While Khalifa was talking to the opium dealer, the man might have seen them from inside the house and had waited until they left. Ajmal saw the man coming out and wanted to talk to him because he had been his permanent customer for several years, but the man had slipped away so fast that Ajmal did not get a chance to say good bye. It surprised Ajmal very much because on previous occasions he would talk to him, sitting on the cot together for a long time. Then Ajmal decided that probably he had had some urgent work to do and did not want to waste time in chit chat.

Khalifa and Peter reached the kitchen. The cook was about to finish his work. The gardener was already waiting in the kitchen. In a few minutes they all went to Khalifa's house. Khalifa was a master in chandu and Peter acted as if he had enough experience with it. The cook and the gardener had never seen how to smoke chandu before, so they were a little excited and a little scared.

All four men made a circle around the chandu pipe. Khalifa chanted a few words and Peter lighted the chandu. Khalifa took a deep puff of chandu smoke and exhaled the smoke in Peter's mouth and Peter into the cook's mouth and the cook into the gardener's mouth. In this way, all four got very intoxicated and dropped on the floor.

In the morning, they all came to their senses. All were very happy and feeling light; all their body aches and pains were gone. They were very refreshed. Khalifa said a few words in praise of chandu which he had learned from his seniors in chandu dens and told them to go to their jobs.

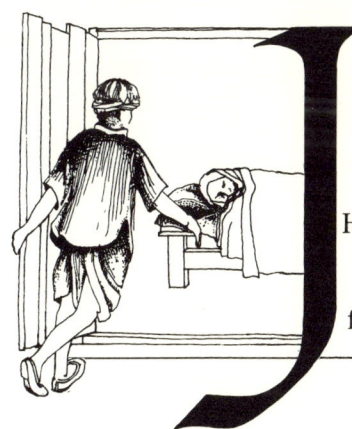

JHABBAN, AFTER LEAVING the mission camp, thought that he should meet his mother and confess all his guilt. He also wanted to meet his mother-in-law for the same purpose. He needed to get to Ranikhet, but he had no money. He did not want to sit on a train without a ticket and he did not want to go back to Dr. Hey to get money from him. He went to the railway station anyhow, and sat down on the curb of a well. He was lost in his thoughts about his past actions and how to get rid of his guilt feelings.

All of a sudden a voice said, "Dr. Peter, why are you sitting here? Do you remember me? I was in your hospital with my foot injury and you cured it. Are you going somewhere by train? I work as a railway coolie here. My hut is nearby. You can sit there while you're waiting."

Peter said, "Yes, I remember you. You had a deep wound. God cured your foot. I am happy to see that your foot is perfect now. I want to go to Kathgodam, but I don't have money to buy a ticket."

The coolie at once said, "Oh, my brother-in-law is a cleaning man on the train and he can take you. The train is ready to go." He took Peter to his brother-in-law and told him how Peter had cured his foot and asked him to take him to Kathgodam. The cleaning man was very happy to meet Peter because he had heard so much about him. Also, for poor people, it is important to have some connection with hospital people. So he took Peter with him very happily.

From Kathgodam Peter took a footpath and reached home in two days. His mother was happy to see Jhabban back, but she still remembered that he had stolen her money. Also, when Jhabban had disappeared, his mother-in-law came to look for him about stealing her money. Both his mother and mother-in-law had had a big fight, so she was still afraid about his habit. Moreover, Jhabban came with empty pockets wearing only a very modern suit and new shiny shoes.

His mother said, "Jhabban, you can live with me, but I am afraid you will steal my money. I am getting old and if I get sick, no one will take care of me if I don't have money. You are a young man. You don't have to worry about your old age. But when you get old, you will also think about having money."

Jhabban very quietly said, "Mother, I am very sorry about

stealing the money. I came here only to ask you to forgive me. I don't need money. So you should not worry that I'll run away with your money. I am also feeling very guilty about stealing my mother-in-law's money, although I sent her four times more money. I want to go there and request her to forgive me. Mother, you know I was addicted to chandu and to get chandu, I started stealing money. Now I don't smoke chandu so I don't need money."

Jhabban's mother's heart began to melt and she hugged her son with tears in her eyes. She said, "Everything is yours, Jhabban. Now take your job again. I have collected enough money to get you remarried." She took out her earthen pot filled with money and said, "Look, I have so much money; you can get a most beautiful woman with this money. You don't have to go to your mother-in-law's house. Your wife Jhumko is already remarried. You have paid four times more money to Gyano so why do you want to go there?"

Jhabban said, "Mother, I want to meet Gyano and get rid of my guilt feelings by confessing to her. I have nothing else to do there. I'll be back very soon."

The next day Jhabban left for his mother-in-law's house. By chance, Jhumko had also come there with her new husband on the same day. Her new husband was a tall, cruel man. He did not hesitate to beat Jhumko and if Gyano would take Jhumko's side, he would beat her, too. So Gyano was very afraid of him, and she was very happy to see Jhabban. Both parties arrived together, so she did not know how to react. Jhabban felt her inconvenience and said, "Gyano, I stole your money. I did it because I had a bad habit of smoking chandu. I want you to forgive me."

Gyano had already received four times more money so she was very happy about it. She could not understand why Jhabban wanted to be forgiven when he had paid her back four times over. She thought that probably Jhabban was very rich and wanted to give her more money or wanted to get Jhumko back. Greed began to hover in her mind like a cloud and she started thinking of a way to steal Jhabban's money. She was afraid of Jhumko's new husband and she wanted to make him happy, so without saying anything to Jhabban she came to Jhumko's husband and took him to her room. Jhumko was also very afraid of her new husband and wanted to go back to Jhabban, but she feared her husband too much. He was a very cruel man and often would tie her to a tree and beat her.

While Gyano was talking to Jhumko's new husband, Jhumko got a chance and she whispered, "Jhabban, take me away from this beast. He will kill me."

Jhabban was a kind man and it did not take him much time to understand when he saw the attitude of Jhumko's new husband that he was very cruel to her. He began to think that if Jhumko wanted to accept him, he would take her back.

Inside the room, Gyano and Jhumko's new husband talked very secretly and they both came out with serious faces. Now Gyano asked Jhabban to come in and join the family in her room. They all talked of different things—about their jobs, sicknesses, money. Jhabban felt very uncomfortable with them and wanted to leave.

He bowed to Gyano and said, "Now I am going back to my house. I must start now. Otherwise, it will be too dark." Gyano said, "You came here after such a long time and are leaving so early. At least stay here for a night. If Jhumko is married to another man, it doesn't mean that you can't stay here. Jhumko's new husband is a very good man and he also wants you to stay."

Jhabban did not want to stay but could not say no. He said, "All right, I'll stay in your deserted chicken coop. I like to sleep outside in the open air."

Gyano cooked delicious food and tried her best to please Jhabban. After taking food, they started talking and again Jhabban became uncomfortable and he left to go to bed.

At night when everyone was asleep Jhumko silently came to the chicken coop and shook Jhabban's arm. Jhabban awoke with a start and saw Jhumko standing by his side. He thought that Jhumko was ready to leave with him, so he at once stood up. Jhumko whispered, "Run away from here. My mother and my husband have planned to rob you. Probably they will kill you." And she disappeared in the dark.

Jhabban already had had some suspicions about their activities so he did not waste time there. He immediately grabbed his things and left the chicken coop.

When Jhabban had run far away, he heard Jhumko screaming and her husband yelling, "You daughter of a bitch! You told him to run away. Now I'll kill you in place of him."

In the dark, Jhabban walked fast without thinking where he was going. When it was morning, he recognized that he was somewhere near the same river. He walked faster and faster and finally reached the same place where he had rested under a tree a few years before.

He sat down again under the same tree. This time he was not afraid of people. He had no money, and it was daylight so Gyano and her new son-in-law couldn't chase him. After resting for an hour, he took a bath in the river and started climbing up the mountain. He reached the same village and met the same people. The children were much bigger, but the adults were the same.

The villagers also recognized him and took him to their hut. Jhabban said to himself that the last time he was sick and had had no choice except to rest in their hut. This time he was not sick and he should not hide that he was from a sweeper family, and if they got upset then he should leave for some other place.

Jhabban said, "I came here to tell you that I am from a sweeper family and I don't want to go inside your huts. You don't know who I am, but I don't feel it right not to tell you the truth."

The villagers at once became silent, as if something terrible had happened. Then one young man said, "I was in the hospital and the man who served me food was a sweeper. If we can sit with a sweeper in a hospital, then why can't we sit with a sweeper in a hut? I think all poor people belong to one caste and all rich people belong to another caste. You are our brother. Don't hesitate to sit with us in our huts." The young man pulled him inside and all the villagers accepted his action by remaining silent.

Jhabban wanted to go to Ranikhet to be with his mother, but the villagers dissuaded him for three days; finally he told them that he could not stay any longer and left. He was not very far from Ranikhet. It was only ten miles by footpath. So he arrived home in three or four hours.

Jhabban's mother had become very sick the same night that Jhabban left for Gyano's house. When he came back, he found his mother on her last breath. She was not able to talk to him. Her speech was stopped and in a few short minutes she died.

Jhabban was very shocked by his mother's sudden death. He could not understand how it happened. He asked his neighbors to help him with her burial ceremony. The street rights which belonged to his mother had no sweeper. When the dwellers of the street heard that Jhabban was back, they came to see him and asked him to resume his hereditary job. Jhabban wanted to serve people by sweeping the street, houses and latrines, but he thought that he could serve mankind much more by doing other things. So he told them that he would forego his hereditary rights of sweeping their street and they could arrange for someone else to take that job.

Now Jhabban had to face the question of what to do. Would he go back to the mission camp? Would he look for a job somewhere in a hospital? His mind could not decide. All of a sudden he remembered that his mother had some money and that he could make good use of it. He could go to some poor labor colony and start giving medicine to sick people. He would spend his mother's money to purchase medicine. When those people earned money, they would pay him back if they could. He had full faith that poor people would benefit from his help.

Jhabban's last attachment was his mother and she was no longer in the world. He had no house or land of his own. He was completely free from all attachment now.

The next morning Jhabban took his mother's savings and left everything else as it was. He told the new man who got his mother's job that he could use the house and everything in it. Then he took a bus to Kathgodam, and from Kathgodam he went to Bareilly. He arrived there at night and slept in a corner of the railway station.

Early in the morning Jhabban woke up and walked to the countryside. The villagers were coming on their bicycles with big cans of milk hanging on both sides to sell in the town. Women were walking fast with loads of sugar cane on their heads. Bullock carts full of cane were going to the sugar factories. The road was very busy in the morning, because after the sun rises high, it gets very hot; everyone was trying to reach the town as early as possible.

Jhabban walked until noon and then it was impossible to walk any further. The road was burning with heat, so Jhabban decided to rest in the shade of a tree. He sat down under a tree and rested until three o'clock. He decided to go as far as some village and stay there for a night. When he resumed his journey, a milkman came by on his bicycle and stopped in front of Jhabban. The man said, "Are you going to Ratlam village?"

Jhabban had no definite plan to go to any particular village, but he said yes. The milkman said, "Then you can ride on the back of my cycle if you want." Jhabban leaped on the back of the bicycle, where two empty milk cans were hanging on each side. It was an uncomfortable ride on a dirt road with two milk cans rattling back and forth. But Jhabban wanted to reach a place where he could stay, so he did not mind all the noise and bumping his buttocks on the iron carrier of the bicycle.

On the way the milkman asked his name. Jhabban said, "Peter." The milkman said, "Then you must be a Christian and Ratlam is a village where only Hindus live. How can you stay there?" Peter said, "I only have to stay one night, and in the morning I'll go somewhere else where people need me."

The milkman was very surprised to hear his answer. He said, "Does that mean you don't have any definite place to go or that you don't have relatives and friends in Ratlam or in any village nearby?"

Peter said, "Yes, that's right. I belong to the mountains. I came to this side to help the poor who are sick and can't afford medicine or to go to hospitals. I can take care of such people. I don't want to earn money for myself. I only want to serve people."

The milkman was even more surprised to see a man who wanted to serve poor people without desiring anything from them. He thought that Peter was either crazy or a cheat. He decided to take him to his house and find out if he really wanted to help the poor. The bicycle stopped in front of a good-sized house. The walls were made of mud and the roof was thatched with grass. It was very clean and different kinds of flowers were growing on the sides of the footpath. The milkman put his bicycle under a mango tree and took Peter into a room which was kept for guests.

The milkman said, "I am from a Gujar (cowboy) caste. All the villagers here are my caste. They are poor, but they earn their livelihood by selling milk. We all keep our cows together in one place; that way it is easy to clean their place and one person can easily take the cows to graze in the fields. That's why you don't see any cows around here."

The milkman offered a large glass filled with milk to Peter. When Peter finished the milk the milkman said, "Let's go outside. I'll show you the village." They both came out and walked on a path which was covered by green grass; on one side of the path there was a water canal. The path was passing through all the houses which were situated in a large "U" shape.

Each house was separate, with two bedrooms, one living room, a porch, and a garden. In front of the house, banana and papaya trees were growing on the boundary lines. The kitchen was separate and behind the row of all houses. About two hundred yards behind the kitchen there was a barn for cows. A large area was fenced by poles and split bamboo was woven like a basket to make the fence. For each cow there was a place, and all the calves were outside the barn within the fence. Peter and the cow man walked all around the village and then came back to the house.

Peter said, "Your village is very clean. The houses are built systematically. Every house has a flower garden."

The milkman said, "Yes. I started cooperative farming here. I was in the army several years ago and when we lived in different camps, we used to arrange dwellings, footpaths and gardens in a perfect plan. After my release from the army, I did the same thing here. We do everything together: we earn money together, we eat together. We have different houses, but we meet every day in one room. We have a school for children. Now we need someone who knows about medicine to start a dispensary here."

It seemed to Peter that everything was being arranged by itself. Perhaps it was God's will. "People here need me and I need them. It seems that these villagers have a better understanding of how to live in this world, so I can work easily with these people."

Peter said, "I have about a thousand rupees. I donate this money to the cooperative farm to start a dispensary." When the milkman saw a thousand rupees in front of him, he was petrified for a while. He said, "A thousand rupees!" He checked the money to see if it were real or fake. He said, "Is it really your money or did you find it somewhere?" He did not want to ask Peter if he had stolen the money.

Peter said, "Yes, it is my money. My mother died a few days ago and she left this money for me. I want to spend it for some good purpose. Don't be afraid that I snatched someone's money. I know that you are an honest person and you are trying to improve the living of all of your community. I have the same ideas, but I want all poor people of any caste, religion, or sect to be helped."

The milkman said, "Peter, my name is Phool Singh. I am President of this cooperative farm. I am very thankful to God that I met you. Now let's go to take food; afterwards we will decide about the dispensary."

In the cooperative farm there were five families. They all sat down after eating their food and decided that Phool Singh's house should be used as the dispensary and that Phool Singh, with his family, should live in some smaller house. The next day, Phool Singh's family moved into a thatched hut, which became their temporary quarters until a new house could be built.

The dispensary started right away. Peter made a list of medicines needed for wounds, cough, cold, fever, headache, malaria, etc. and Phool Singh brought those things from Bareilly, where he would go every day to sell milk.

Doctors and diseases go together. When there was no doctor, nobody worried about minor diseases, but now, if anyone got a fever, headache or any wound, he would go to Peter and get cured. Gradually, people of other villages heard about Peter, and they also started coming to him. Within a month, Peter became a famous doctor around the villages.

IN THE MISSION camp, Khalifa, Peter, the cook and the gardener had become very close friends. They would smoke chandu every night. When there are several people participating, the cost of chandu is less, and also there is more fun. So all four started converting people into chandu smokers. The school teacher was a religious man. He was old and had backaches. Peter brought him in by telling him that his backache would go away. The school teacher tried chandu and it took away his pain; he felt much stronger. But when he got addicted, his back was more painful if he did not get chandu every day. The cook brought his assistant cook. In this way, the circle had twelve members. All were very serious in their aims. Now the work in the garden was not so good; sometimes the gardener would even forget to water the plants. The cook would forget to put salt in the vegetables, or forget altogether to cook the food. Peter would sleep in his room and did not clean the house properly. The school teacher was more alive than before, but he did not know what he was talking about; he would talk and talk all the time. When patients did not get fed on time, they reported it to Dr. Hey. Dr. Hey noticed that everything was going downhill. He tried his best to improve the working system. He asked everyone to attend church on Sunday morning. He wanted to give a long lecture on aims, ideals, and the purpose of the New Christian Mission.

On Saturday night Khalifa made an extra-strong dose of chandu because on Sunday they had no duties. He forgot about going to church on Sunday morning. On Saturday night, all twelve people amused themselves by singing and dancing until midnight, and then they sat in a circle and smoked chandu as usual. The room was completely calm. The candle took its last breath and died out. The room was filled with darkness.

In the morning the church bell rang and all the people went to the church wearing their best clean clothes. Dr. Hey spoke about the work of the mission and how people were not taking much interest in it. Then he noticed that several men were missing. He asked why those people did not come. Someone said they had been singing in Khalifa's room until midnight.

After completing the prayer, Dr. Hey went to Khalifa's house. He found the twelve men still unconscious. He said to himself, "My worst fears are true. When I saw Peter and Khalifa talking to Ajmal, the opium dealer, I knew there was something going on between them. Now I understand everything." He left the room and went straight to his house. It was Sunday so there was no work for him either. All the chandu smokers came to their senses when the sun was high in the sky. The school teacher said, "It was a strong dose, Khalifa. My head is still aching. I think I should sit in your room until I am able to walk." A few stood up and went home with staggering legs. A few remained sitting, holding their heads between their knees.

Peter was a house worker; for him there was no holiday. It was very late to wash the floor and to dust the room of Dr. Hey. He knew that Dorothy would be very angry at him. So he ran to his duty and at once started cleaning the house. Dorothy came out of her room and said, "Peter, it is eleven o'clock. Where were you? I did not see you in the church either. Now it is time to eat and you are just starting to wash the floor." She did not want to show how angry she was, because she did not want Peter to run away again.

Peter did not say anything. He was feeling guilty about not doing his work on time. Today he was rubbing the floor even harder to make it shiny so that Dr. Hey and Dorothy would be pleased. He finished the floor and cleaned the whole house.

He had never worked so hard before. Dorothy became very happy and said, "Peter, don't feel bad about being late. You have worked so hard today. Now, take your food and rest."

In the evening, Dr. Hey took Peter with him to visit the hospital as usual. Peter did nothing in the hospital, but it was one of his duties to follow Dr. Hey while he visited each patient. After visiting the patients, Dr. Hey took Peter with him for a walk. Peter was afraid that Dr. Hey might go to visit some people in town and come home very late, but he could not say, "I don't want to go very far with you." When it was getting late and Dr. Hey did not show any mood to return, Peter started limping and stopped paying attention to Dr. Hey's talk.

Dr. Hey said, "Why are you limping? You are a young, strong man." Peter said, "It's nothing sir. I twisted my ankle. I guess I had better return if you don't mind." Dr. Hey said, "Yes, we should return and I'll check your ankle. It might be very bad if it is not bandaged immediately. Do you want my arm to help you home?" Peter said, "It's okay. I can walk." They returned to the house and the doctor immediately put hot water fomentation over Peter's ankle. Then he bandaged it and told Peter to rest and not to walk. Peter stood up and said, "It is all cured. I don't feel any pain. Look, I can walk perfectly." The doctor said, "If you don't put pressure on it today, then it will be all right. If you walk, then it will probably give you pain."

Peter left for his room saying, "I'll rest." The doctor knew that Peter's ankle was not twisted. He was only pretending to have pain.

It was almost eight o'clock and Peter secretly left for Khalifa's house. The doctor was waiting for Peter to leave. When he realized that Peter had left, he came out of his room wearing a long black coat and an Indian cap and went to Khalifa's house. Everyone was talking about last night's trip. They started sitting in a circle. The candle was spreading its light dimly so that faces were not seen clearly. Dr. Hey secretly stood outside the door. Everyone was concentrating on chandu. The smoking ritual started and when the smoke reached the men near the door, the doctor slipped in, stretched his neck in the circle and opened his mouth. The puff of smoke went right inside his stomach and then he puffed it out into the next man's mouth.

In a few minutes the ritual was over and the room was filled with silence. In the morning everyone came to their senses and they saw Dr. Hey trying to lift his head. He was still dizzy.

Khalifa said, "How is he here? He was not in the circle last night. Probably he was drunk and came here by mistake." Peter helped the doctor to sit up. Dr. Hey said, "It's much stronger than eating opium. Oh, I liked it. Peter, why didn't you tell me before? I saw you once at Ajmal's house and I knew that something was going on. Oh, I feel so good, as if I am in heaven." Peter was afraid that if Dorothy found out about it she would be very angry. He did not want Dr. Hey to talk about it anymore. He realized that Dr. Hey was talking like an intoxicated man. If he showed signs of intoxication in the house, Dorothy would never forgive them. He did not know that the doctor was an old opium user and that this was his first time to smoke chandu.

Peter said, "Sir, let's go to the house. Can you walk all right?" Dr. Hey said, "I'm all right. I can walk by myself. Let's go." They both left together and on the way Peter said, "Sir, if you want us not to smoke, we will stop it. But don't say anything to your wife. She will be very angry." The doctor said, "Peter, I don't want you to tell my wife anything about me smoking chandu at Khalifa's house. Do you understand?" Peter and the doctor made a pact not to say anything about it in the house.

Everyone was afraid that the doctor would stop the smoking of chandu in the camp. They did not believe that he had smoked chandu with them. They thought that either he came there drunk, or that he came there to find them out and started pretending that he smoked the chandu. In the dim light no one saw him smoking. For the whole day, everyone expected that someone would announce that all those who smoked chandu at Khalifa's house should either stop smoking chandu or leave the camp. Noon passed and no one said anything. Then it was evening and the sun was about to set, and still no one announced anything. Night came and people were beginning to think that probably the doctor would say something the next day, so it might be the last chance. Everyone had the same thought and they came to Khalifa's house to enjoy their last day's chandu ritual at the mission camp. Who knows what would happen tomorrow?

Everyone worried about where they would go if they were not allowed to smoke chandu at Khalifa's house. Some suggested Ajmal's opium den. But that was very costly. It was Ajmal's business and he made much profit from it. Also he bribed the police every month, which he had to include in the price of chandu. At Khalifa's house, it was very cheap, only the cost of chandu stuff which they would bring turn by turn.

Khalifa said, "Let's enjoy today. Why worry for tomorrow? Be happy. Forget everything." People started sitting in the circle.

The doctor ate his supper and announced to his wife that he was going for a walk. He did not want to smoke chandu with his workers, but his desire was pulling him. So he thought that if he could get away for a while, he could forget it. He came out of the compound and started walking as if in a dream and after a while, he found himself sitting in the circle next to Peter just before the ritual was started. In the circle when his turn came, he could not stop his desire and his mouth opened automatically. The ritual was completed and again the room was silent.

In the morning Dr. Hey stood up as soon as he came to his senses and left for his house. The others came to their senses gradually. Some left and some remained sitting for some time.

Khalifa had not noticed that the doctor was also in the circle. Only three or four people in the circle who were sitting close to the doctor knew about it.

Chandu smokers don't get excited about anything. They are half asleep all the time. When they knew the doctor was in the circle, it did not make them very happy. For them it seemed normal, but the fear of prohibition of chandu smoking in the camp was much less that day. No one talked about it. All of a sudden there was a big change in the mission camp.

The hospital was filled with patients, but they were not real patients. They were chandu smokers but were shown as patients in the hospital register. The hospital was a big source of revenue for the mission. Also the rate of converting people to Christianity was increased. Chandu addicts would happily accept any religion to get chandu. For them, no religion, sect or God—nothing was greater than chandu.

Dr. Hey was much respected by the authorities of the New Christian Mission, because the hospital register showed good progress and the church register showed great progress in converting people to Christianity.

Dr. Hey himself was very happy because he no longer had to worry about the patients, since they were not real patients. People were accepting Christianity. This was his main aim and he was getting chandu every day. People were going to church for hours at a time. Whether they listened or not, they could sit and sleep on the chairs. He only wanted the number of people attending church to increase.

Khalifa had never been accepted by people anywhere in his life. This was the first time anyone asked his opinion when Dr. Hey called him to his house and said, "Khalifa, you are a Christian and a permanent member of the mission. We are getting more and more people and we can't accommodate them here. I am afraid that if more people start coming, your room will not be large enough. People have already taken over the whole hospital—people are staying at the school building. What should we do?" Khalifa's mind had burned out long ago. He only knew how to make chandu. He said, "Sir, I don't know what to do. If I don't have to do anything else, then I can arrange for some people to smoke in the morning and some at night."

Dr. Hey thought that this was a good plan. He only wanted to fill his registers with the names of different people. If Khalifa started two shifts, then it would help a lot.

In the register, the mission camp showed great progress. Its membership had increased, but inside there was nothing happening except chandu smoking. Dorothy was happy because the report from the authorities was very good. In the church more people were coming for prayer. The doctor was also happy, partly due to smoking chandu and partly because he had no work in the hospital. He filled the register with patients from his own smoking room.

IN RATLAM VILLAGE, Phool Singh and Peter (Jhabban) worked hard to make the dispensary successful. Patients began to pour in. From morning to night Peter had no time to do anything but take care of the patients. He was very polite, kind and ready to serve people day and night; so everyone who came to him became his friend. The patients would say, "Peter has magic in his hands. If he touches a patient, he starts getting cured."

Several villages including Ratlam were owned by a landlord whose ancestors were once kings. This landlord had some skin disease on his arm. Several doctors had given him medicine, but it was never cured. When he heard the praise of Peter, he called him to come to his house. Peter considered that if he walked ten miles, it would mean the loss of three hours. In three hours he could serve lots of poor people. So he told the messenger that he had no time to go there. If the landlord had time, then he could come to Ratlam.

The landlord did not like this news, but he figured that if he was cured by Peter's medicine, then it would be forgivable. Otherwise, he would kick him out of the village for disobeying him. The next morning the landlord arrived and Peter examined his arm. He could not understand the disease. He had never seen that kind of skin disease before. He very politely said, "Sir, I don't know how to cure it. It seems it is a very old disease." The landlord was already angry because Peter had not come to his house and now he clearly said he didn't know what to do about it. The landlord burst with anger and said, "You cheat. You are sitting here to cheat these poor people. If you don't know about a disease, then why are you sitting here?" Peter remained very calm and said, "Sir, I can make a medicine. It will probably work, but I am not sure." The landlord cooled down and said, "Do you need money to make that medicine?" Peter said, "No. I need two pounds of garlic and one pound of butter. I have a few herbs here. I'll make it tonight and tomorrow I can apply the medicine." The landlord sent the required things and the next day he again went to see Peter.

Peter was busy with other patients and when the landlord's turn came, he took a bottle of ointment. He cleaned the skin with garlic juice and then put on the ointment and told the landlord to take the ointment and put it on every day after cleaning the skin with garlic juice. He said to show him his arms after seven days.

Peter was so busy with his work that he almost forgot about the landlord. When Phool Singh and the others heard that the landlord was angry at Peter, they thought that Peter had been disrespectful to the landlord and that he should have gone to the landlord's house. At night they talked to Peter and told him that he should go to the landlord's house on the seventh day to check. Peter said nothing, but he did not want to go to the landlord just because he was rich. For Peter all patients were the same, rich or poor, of any caste or religion. Early in the morning of the seventh day, while Peter sat in his chair, he saw the landlord standing in front of the line. Peter checked his skin and said, "It's cured." The landlord laughed and said, "I know it's cured. That's why I came so early, to show you. I heard very much about you from villagers, but I didn't believe that you really had a healing power. I know it was not the medicine which cured me. It's your own healing power."

Peter did not have much time to talk to him so he smilingly said, "A doctor is a patient's friend as long as the sickness is not cured. Now I have to see my other friends," and he continued giving medicine to other patients. The landlord left the room and sat down in the shade of a tree. He was a little confused because Peter was not taking any special interest in him, as if he were the same as the other patients. He very much wanted to talk to Peter because he was very happy to be cured. At noon, Peter came out of his room and saw the landlord still sitting under the tree. He went to him and said, "You came so early in the morning and you are still here. I think you have not taken your food yet. I hope you will not mind taking your meal with me."

The landlord stood up and said, "Peter, let's go into your room. I want to talk to you," and they both sat down in the room. Peter offered the landlord food and milk. After eating, the landlord said, "I want to donate a huge amount of money to you. It is my great desire. I hope you will not reject it."

Peter did not want any money for himself, but he thought that if the landlord made a hospital, it would help poor people. So he told the landlord to build a hospital with that money. The landlord agreed to it and left. At night, when all the co-operative farm people were collected, Peter told them the desire of the landlord to build a hospital. Phool Singh and his friends were very happy about it. The next morning Phool Singh went straight to the landlord to thank him for his offer to build a hospital. The landlord said, "It was Peter's desire to build the hospital. He doesn't want money for himself. In fact, I have donated money to Peter, and Peter donated it to build a hospital." Phool Singh said, "But the money is yours and the building should be in your name," and so saying, he returned to his house somewhat disturbed.

Peter's fame was increasing so fast that it was bothering the cooperative farm members. Outwardly, they were quite friendly to Peter. Phool Singh would easily get upset if Peter did not do something according to his wishes. It hurt his ego of presidentship.

The construction of the hospital building started and several poor people in the village got jobs in their own village. The construction work was going very fast because the villagers who were working thought of it as their own thing. The walls were made with rocks and mud and the roof was made out of corrugated tin. In a few months, the building was all completed and Peter shifted his work to the new building.

The landlord had faith in Peter's work, but he wanted some trained doctor to be sent by the government. So he explained the need of a doctor to the government and requested that someone be sent as early as possible. The government sent a doctor to Ratlam hospital because there was a real need there. The hospital was already functioning, so it was easy for a doctor to assume his duty.

Now Ratlam hospital was a government-aided hospital. All the staff there were government servants and received salaries. Peter had no desire to get a salary. He wanted to serve the poor. For some reason he believed that if he accepted a salary, he could not cure people.

During these five or six months, the mission camp was completely changed. Somehow the police found out that it was used as a chandu den, so one night when all were unconscious from smoking, the police arrested them. Fortunately, Dr. Hey was not there that night since he had taken his chandu in the day shift. Khalifa, Peter and the others all went to prison. Only a few new people were left at the camp. Now Dr. Hey's eyes were opened. He was preaching one thing and doing something else. He said to himself, "Honesty, kindness and compassion are not the property of any one religion. No religion can own those qualities. Individually a person can be honest, kind, compassionate. I was in great ignorance and I was taking everyone into ignorance. In fact, I am responsible for all this corruption, dishonesty and the usage of chandu. I have to confess my guilt in front of God."

On Sunday, a high priest came to the church for a service. When the priest had completed his sermon, Dr. Hey stood up and said, "I want to confess all my guilt in front of the priest and the public. I, myself, was involved in smoking chandu, which was the cause of the destruction of the hospital, school and mission activities. All those names which are shown as converted Christians are not real converts. They are all chandu smokers, and I know that chandu addicts don't have any religion. Their only religion is to obtain chandu."

The head priest was a kind old man and when he heard Dr. Hey taking all the blame on himself, he said, "God is merciful and He forgives one who confesses his sins in front of Him."

Church was over and people went home. Dorothy was very shocked to hear that her husband was also a chandu smoker. She did not say anything to her husband. Dr. Hey felt her pain, but he could do nothing about the past. To him, confession was important. He did not want to hide his sins and feel guilty for the rest of his life.

That night, Dorothy went to bed early, and Dr. Hey opened a book in his reading room. In the morning Dorothy made tea for him, but he was neither in his bed nor in his office. She looked all around and then thought, "Probably he was sad and could not sleep, so maybe he has gone for a walk." For a long time she waited and then asked others if anyone had seen him. She was still expecting him, but the day passed. Several days passed and still her husband did not return.

Dorothy was a brave lady and she wanted to make the work started by her husband successful, so she took all responsibility into her own hands and began to work hard.

Once a religious work gets a bad reputation, it is very difficult to get it running smoothly again. All the chandu smokers who weren't arrested left, because they were addicted and there was no way to use chandu at the camp any more. Only a few people, mostly women, remained there. The hospital was completely vacant. There were no patients, no workers and no doctor.

Dorothy was a wise woman. She changed the mission camp into an orphan's child care center. Male energy was not essential in taking care of children, and there were four or five women who were very honest and sincere workers. They had a few children of their own who were not orphans but who had no fathers. So the child care began to function immediately with their own children; gradually they began to receive children from hospitals of unwed mothers or from the police, who picked up children abandoned on the streets by their impoverished parents.

Dorothy and a few women would make a tour around the city every day and if they received news of a needy child anywhere, they would bring it to the center. Within a few months, the center was filled with ten children, excluding their own.

The authorities of the New Christian Mission were unhappy about Dr. Hey's disappearance because he was the person who had started the mission camp in Bareilly. They had much hope and expectations of him, but all of a sudden, he had disappeared. They never blamed him for chandu smoking; they wanted to cover up the whole matter somehow and let the camp carry on as it had been functioning. The child care center was not very attractive work for them, but the money which was granted for the hospital was transferred to the child care so that the mission would remain alive in some form.

NOW IN RATLAM HOSPITAL, patients began to pour in. The doctor there was a young man who came directly from college. He had no practical experience in a hospital. Most of the time he would get upset from seeing so many patients, and sometimes he would get angry with the patients if they asked for certain help. Peter felt very badly to see the attitude of the doctor toward the patients, but he was a subordinate and not even a nurse. In the register of the hospital he was a ward boy, although he was respected by the patients much more than the doctor. This was one of the reasons that the doctor was upset. He could not tolerate that a ward boy should be respected more than he, himself.

When the doctor learned that his attitude toward the patients bothered Peter, he started showing even more anger. Sometimes in front of patients he would order Peter to clean the floor to show his superiority. Peter would clean the floor, clean the pots, change bed sheets. He enjoyed serving patients and patients enjoyed being with him.

Peter tried his best to please the doctor so that the work in the hospital would run smoothly, but the doctor suspected that Peter was trying to please him to get his special favor.

Phool Singh was happy to see the hospital and felt proud to be a friend of a doctor; he went to the doctor's house in the evening to play cards. When Phool Singh learned that the doctor was very unhappy with Peter, he also started avoiding Peter. He had been in the army so he knew that a doctor is a big man. To be a friend of a doctor meant one gained much respect. He also thought that it is the medicine which cures a patient. The doctor knew all about medicines, so he was more important for the hospital than Peter, who was not really a doctor.

One day the doctor said, "Peter you are a ward boy. The government pays you for your job. The government can't allow any person to work in the hospital who doesn't accept wages. So either accept your wages or leave the hospital. I understand why you don't accept the wages. It is because you don't want to be called a ward boy. You want to work as a doctor."

To Peter, a ward boy, a doctor and a sweeper were the same. All were serving patients in their own ways. He was not proud to be called a doctor and was not ashamed to be called a ward boy or sweeper.

Phool Singh was standing beside the doctor, and he was getting more upset than the doctor. He at once said, "Doctor, I brought Peter to this village and Peter started a dispensary in my house. In fact, he donated a thousand rupees to the cooperative farm for this purpose. Probably Peter feels that he has a claim over this hospital. The cooperative farm can return his money if you want him to leave the hospital."

Peter said, "Sir, it's time to serve the patients. I have to go now. I understand what you mean," and he left for his duty. The doctor murmured when he left, "Damn fool, causing trouble in the hospital," and he left for his office.

Phool Singh remained standing alone. He could not understand why the doctor was so angry at Peter. Peter was not doing anything wrong. But he thought that if Peter didn't leave the hospital, then the doctor would surely create a problem, which would mean a great loss to the village.

At night, when cooperative farm members were collected to eat, Phool Singh announced that Peter's money should be returned since the dispensary had merged into the hospital, and the government had already paid back the money they had invested in the dispensary. Everyone accepted the proposal because they were jealous of Peter's reputation; so Phool Singh took the money to give to Peter. But he was afraid to give the money back—he knew that Peter would not accept it. Also, returning the money meant telling him to leave. Phool Singh, who had been previously favoring the doctor, changed his mind. He began to see the honesty, sincerity and love in Peter. He decided to put the money in Peter's bag secretly. If he left, he would take the bag and if he didn't leave, he was not going to open his bag, since there was nothing in it except one old shirt with several patches.

Phool Singh put the money in his bag when Peter was eating and left the room. At midnight, Peter decided to leave. He took his bag and opened it. He found one thousand rupees in it. He understood that it meant, "Peter, leave the village." Then he said to himself, "This money belongs to the cooperative farm to which I donated it. If I take this money, I would be stealing." He took his shirt out of the bag and left the bag in the room.

In the morning Peter was not on duty. The patients became impatient when they heard that Peter was not there. They were very attached to him and began to wonder if he were sick or whether something bad had happened to him.

Phool Singh also heard about his absence, and he felt very bad to lose Peter. Also he felt guilty about showing his anger towards Peter to please the doctor. But he felt good that Peter had enough money to go anywhere he wanted. He went to Peter's room to clean it so that he could use it for an office. He saw the bag sitting in its own place and thought that probably Peter had not left. He picked up the bag and opened it. The money was there completely untouched, but Peter's shirt was not there. Phool Singh said, "What an honest man. He is a saint. He is not an ordinary person. I lost the diamond for a piece of glass. Can I find him again? At least his foot steps in Ratlam have made a hospital. We got what we deserved. We can't get more because we don't deserve any more. That's why he left."

The doctor was very happy. Peter was like a huge boulder blocking his fame. Now his path was clear. He went to visit the patients in the hospital. Every patient he visited asked him about Peter. Some of the patients even guessed that the doctor was very jealous of him and that this could be the cause of Peter's departure. Some patients hated the doctor because of his nasty nature and they immediately left the hospital.

A snake that loses its gem becomes an ordinary snake. Peter was the gem of the hospital. Its fame was due to Peter. As soon as he left, the glow of the hospital faded away. The patients began to leave and very few new patients came for treatment. The doctor tried his best to impress people. He became very polite; he even started acting like Peter, but all in vain.

Peter walked all night. He reached the main road and started walking fast. It was still dark, but villagers were going to town to sell milk on their bicycles. Peter did not want to be recognized by the villagers. He knew that if anyone saw him leaving, they would not let him go; so he changed his direction and went into the woods, which belonged to a forest plantation. There was a path in the middle of the plantation and Peter started following it all alone. On the way he began to think about his future. Should he go to the mission camp again and get trapped in religious fanaticism? Should he go to Ranikhet and resume his hereditary rights of sweeping and live without worry? Should he go to the cities and beg food and do nothing? Walking slowly and sometimes resting in the shade of trees, Peter again reached Bareilly. He was hungry and tired. He had no money to buy food, but he had never begged for food before, so he was ashamed to do that. But hunger was chewing his intestines so he decided to beg. It was night and the shopkeepers were ready to close their shops. A vegetable seller collected his good vegetables, put them in a basket and threw away a bunch of carrots on the street. Peter picked up the carrots and thought it was God's grace that he had found so many carrots, sufficient for two meals. He went to a well and washed the carrots; he sat down on the railing of the well and began to eat them. When a person is very hungry, everything tastes good. These carrots had been freshly picked in a vegetable garden that very morning. Carrots were so abundant in the marketplace that there was no hope of selling all of them. So it was useless for the shopkeeper to carry so great a load. That was the reason he had thrown them away. Peter ate more than half of the carrots, and then he wanted to go to sleep in some safe, secluded place. He looked at a few spots but could not find a good place to sleep. He went back to the railway station, where he could find a buggy in the yard waiting to be washed. He knew that poor railway coolies slept in those buggies at night. He found one buggy, but it was filled with railway coolies. He climbed in anyway and chose a corner to sleep in, curling up into a circle. There was a beggar curled up near him and when he heard someone sit down, he lifted his head still covered with a towel and peaked through a hole in the towel with one eye. He saw a man carrying a bunch of carrots. His hunger began to grind his intestines and he said, "Please sir, give me food. I am hungry."

Peter knew what hunger feels like, so he gave the bunch of carrots to the beggar. The beggar began to eat, chewing loudly. It sounded like an elephant walking on dry twigs. It was so loud that the coolies who were trying to sleep heard it. One of them yelled, "You stupid beggars. Get out of here. It's not for you to sleep here. We work all day and at night you disturb our sleep." He stood up and pushed the beggar out of the buggy and then he turned to Peter and said, "One more is still hiding. Get out, stupid!" He dragged him by the arm and threw him out. Peter wandered back to the streets and found a corner to curl up in. He slept soundly. In the morning, as the sun was about to rise, a cool breeze was blowing; it comforted Peter and he fell deeper and deeper into sleep.

As Dorothy and her friends were making their rounds of the city, they came by chance to the street where Peter was sleeping. They saw a man lying in a corner and thought that either he was dead or sick. Dorothy at once went to him and tried to check his heartbeat. Peter opened his eyes and, seeing a woman bending over him, he at once sat up with a start. Dorothy said, "Peter, what are you doing here? When were you released from the prison? Where are the others?"

Peter did not understand what she was talking about. He said, "How is Dr. Hey?" Dorothy said, "Oh, after you were taken to prison, Dr. Hey also disappeared. Now the hospital is closed and we have a child care center and a school for children."

Peter said, "I was not taken to prison. I was always free. I am still free." Dorothy and her friends guessed that Peter had gone mad due to his chandu smoking. They figured that was the reason he was sleeping in this corner—no sane man would sleep here. It was useless to argue with him, and if he came to the child care center, he could make trouble again. So Dorothy and her friends left immediately.

Peter stood up and dusted his old shirt, which he used to sleep on; he went to a well to wash his hands and face. Then he sat down near the well to rest for some time and decide where to go. He had a desire to meet Doctor Hey, who was really a good man, but he felt uncomfortable about the doctor's obsession of converting people to Christianity. Otherwise, he was kind, compassionate, a hard worker and a friend of the poor. Peter did not want to go back to the mission camp. He decided to go somewhere in the mountains where people were simple, honest and hard working. Besides, mountain towns were not crowded like cities. But finding food in the mountains was not easy, and life was very difficult due to the cold.

Peter went to the railway station to see if he could get a ride to some place. By chance, the very same man who had once taken Peter with him on the train was putting oil in the wheels of an engine. As Peter walked by, unattentive to the outer world, the man noticed him and whistled to get his attention. Peter looked up and recognized him. The man said, "Peter, where are you going? I work on this engine now. I am going to Dehradun. If you want, I can take you there. You can sit in the engine with me."

Peter was surprised by how fast God arranged everything. He said, "Yes, I want to go to the mountains. I am fed up with the noise of the cities. I know that from Dehradun I can easily go to Mussoori. I'll be very thankful to you if you take me to Dehradun." The oilman washed his hands at once and climbed in the engine, asking Peter to come in. He made tea and they both sat down to bread and tea. Peter was a little afraid that the engineer would not allow him to ride in the engine. The engineer came and the oilman introduced him as Dr. Peter. The driver was a humorous man. He said, "From which college did you graduate? I have never seen any doctor like you, wearing such dirty clothes. Can you cure my arm?" He rolled up his sleeve and said, "This is some kind of skin disease. I have used several medicines and nothing helped. You are a doctor. Maybe you can do something for it."

Peter said, "I can make a medicine, but it is God who cures through the medicine." He asked for garlic and butter. The oilman brought everything Peter asked for and in a couple of hours, the ointment was ready. Peter put the ointment on the engineer's arm very gently and wrapped it up with a cloth. The engineer did not take the medicine very seriously. He was only amusing himself by talking to Peter. He had no faith in such medicine, because when so many doctors had not been able to cure him with costly medicine, how could this handmade ointment cure him? The driver smiled and said, "Doctor, what is your fee?"

The oilman said, "Sir, can you allow him to ride in the engine? He wants to go to Dehradun." The driver said, "Oh, that's what the medicine is for! All right, Dr. Peter, I'll take you to Dehradun, but only if you don't charge me your fee," and he laughed again.

In the evening, the train left for Dehradun. On the way the driver amused himself by telling stories and sometimes making fun of Peter, or the oilman, or his assistant. He told a story about when he was driving a passenger train and it crashed with a goods train near Lucknow. He had jumped out of the running train. Several hundred people were killed and the villagers nearby started to loot the train. He had been injured but still he stopped the villagers from looting the train. He told another story of gangsters who jumped in the engine and tied him down and hijacked the whole train. Somehow he had managed to free himself and, grabbing a huge piece of charcoal, he hit the man who had taken control of the engine. He saved the life of several people that day, fighting single-handed with the gangsters. For his bravery he was given a reward.

His assistant, the oilman and the orderly had heard these stories every day, but they pretended as if they enjoyed them because the driver would allow their friends to sit in the engine and to travel free of charge. He would also take his whole crew to the restaurant for tea, and sometimes he would even pay for their food. The next day the train reached Dehradun and Peter said, "Sir, may I check your arm before I leave?" The driver laughed and said, "Oh sure, you can check, after all, you are a doctor. It is your duty to take care of your patient."

Peter took the bandage off and there was no sign of skin disease. The driver could not believe it. He said, "Is it really cured? Maybe it will flare up again." Peter said, "Sir, the ointment is with your oilman. Use it for a few more days and, if God wishes, the problem will completely go away."

The driver was very happy to see this miracle. He could hardly believe that someone who had never gone to school and had never studied medicine could cure a sickness. While he was looking at his arm, Peter said, "Sir, I'm leaving now. I have to go to Mussoori." The driver said, "If you don't have any place there, you could stay with my parents. I can give you their address. Let's go to the rest house first. We will bathe and take some food first."

The driver took Peter to his rest house and gave him new clothes to wear and a thick blanket to protect himself from the cold. After his supper, he took Peter to a motor station and bought a ticket for him for Mussoori.

PETER HAD THE ADDRESS of the humorous engineer's parents but he thought that if he stayed there he could not live freely, so when he reached Mussoori he went instead to the sweepers' colony. He had clean clothing; he had lived with well educated people and could speak in a civilized manner, so the sweepers showed him much respect and asked if he needed any help. Peter only wanted a place to stay, so he asked if there were any place where he could live. The sweepers said, "There is no separate room in our colony except a deserted chicken coop. You can either live with one of us, or if you want to live by yourself, then we can fix up that chicken coop for you. During winters it is very cold here and sometimes it snows four to five feet. At that time, you can move into our houses." Peter said, "I'll be glad to live in the chicken coop. I'll need some help to fix it." Some young boys said, "We will help you, brother, don't worry." They quickly cleaned the coop, fixed it with doors, nailed a tin sheet over the roof and patched the holes in the sides. In a few hours, the chicken coop was turned into Peter's room. Peter had no money, but he wanted to give something to the boys who had worked so hard in fixing his room. He at once took off his clothes and said, "Sell these clothes and distribute the money among yourselves," and he put on the old patched shirt which he always kept with him.

At first, the boys thought that he was joking, but when they realized that he really wanted to give his clothes away, they could not decide whether to take them or not. Peter realized their hesitation and said, "If you don't take them, I'll give them to someone else. I don't need clothes." The boys at once grabbed the clothes and left for the market to sell them.

No one asked Peter's name and Peter did not tell it to anyone. He sat down in his room; it was nothing more than a big box, and there was no light. But for Peter it was pretty large, and big enough to sleep in comfortably, because he was only five feet tall. For a bed, the boys had brought enough dry grass to lie on. If the doors were closed, it was not cold at all.

The next morning Peter woke up and went to the village church. He cleaned the porch, yard and floor of the church. The people going to church thought he might be crazy. He was wearing a shirt and a loin cloth and sweeping the yard without having been asked to do so. But they liked his work and gave him some food. They did not talk to him because if he were crazy he might start cursing them. After he had cleaned the church, Peter went to his room and sat down with his door closed. In the evening, he again came out and went to a temple. He cleaned the floor, worked in the garden and repaired the path. The people in the temple thought that he must be some devotee of God and so they offered him food, sweets and fruits. When it got dark Peter left for his room.

He repeated the same routine every day and within a month he was well known in Mussoori by the name of Bhagatji.*

Everybody in town knew that Bhagatji cleaned churches, temples, mosques and the worshiping places of all faiths, and that he himself lived in a colony of untouchables, in a small chicken coop. Their respect for Bhagatji began to increase.

When people see a person who is devoted to God, they presume that through his grace, any sickness can be cured. So sometimes women would bring their sick babies to be touched by Bhagatji and the babies would get well. Gradually, sick children began to come to him, and then sick adults started coming. Bhagatji would tell them that God would cure them and sometimes he would suggest some medicine. Sometimes he would give them some leaf, root, or flower to eat.

Bhagatji's healing power was now greater than before. His mind was not at all in wordly things. He was not aware of his powers. That he would help everyone was the normal course for him. But people were getting cured and everyone realized that Bhagatji had healing powers. Sometimes people were confused by him. He was so unconcerned about his behavior that some people thought he was crazy. Moreover, he did not talk; he would reply yes or no by nodding his head.

In those very days when Bhagatji was famous as a healer, there was another odd doctor who would see patients and would not charge a fee. He never came out of his room. Sometimes he would pray to God for hours to cure a patient, and sometimes he would sit silently and write down formulas for medicines. The people living near him would bring him food and clothes and clean his room. They had much respect for him because he was a doctor and also a foreigner. This doctor heard about Bhagatji's healing powers and wanted to meet him, but he would not come out of his room, and Bhagatji would not go inside anyone's house. It did not seem possible for them to meet.

---

* Bhagatji means "devout person".

Bhagatji's emotional state was changing very fast. He had stopped talking and was eating very little. He worked cleaning temples, churches, mosques and streets and did not pay attention to the public. One day, while he was sweeping a gutter by the side of a street, a woman crying very piteously came out of her house with a child in her arms. Bhagatji was working right below the door steps. The woman came out in the street and stood in front of Bhagatji. Bhagatji stood up to straighten his back and the woman put the child in his arms. The baby was dead. Bhagatji did not understand what was happening at first, and then he looked at the child. He slowly walked away with the dead child in his arms, and the weeping mother followed him. Seeing this scene, several people followed them and gradually it became a procession. A few people said, "The child must be a great soul. Look, Bhagatji is carrying him in his arms to give the last rites burial ceremony." But Bhagatji slowly turned toward his chicken coop instead of going to the burial place. When he arrived at his room, he went in with the baby in his arms and closed the door. The public stayed outside, waiting to see what would happen next. The mother was in much pain and still crying. She did not know what to do—whether to stay there until Bhagatji opened the door, or whether to ask Bhagatji to give her dead child back for burial. An hour passed and people were getting impatient. The mother rushed to the doors to knock, when she heard the baby crying. "Is he alive?" she said to herself. She heard again the cry of her baby and she screamed, "My baby is alive! Bhagatji! Open the door!"

Bhagatji opened the door and the mother quickly picked up the baby from Bhagatji's lap and ran away to her house. The public was very amazed that the dead child got life from Bhagatji, and someone asked, "What did he do inside the room?" Someone replied, "Maybe prayer or maybe some herb that he put in the baby's mouth." Some said, "God is within Bhagatji. His touch is enough to heal the sicknesses."

Bhagatji closed his door and the people slowly left. He sat down on his bed and began to think. "Oh, even compassion, kindness and helping others is a desire. That desire is also a trap. Imprisonment in a house or in a palace is the same because in both places the desire of getting free is the same.

"To find complete freedom I have to go beyond desires. I have nothing left in the world. I want to dive and dissolve in the ocean of peace."

His mind began to turn inward and he lost consciousness of the body and world. He was completely in a state of deep trance.

When he came to his senses he found that he had no desire to communicate to the outer world in any way. From that day no one saw Bhagatji—neither in the church, nor in the temple. He stopped going out of his room. The sweepers would bring him food and he wanted nothing else.

ONE DAY all the chandu smokers were released from Bareilly prison. By now Khalifa and Peter were intimate friends and they wanted to stay together. The others left for their homes. Peter and Khalifa wanted to leave Bareilly, so they went to the railway station. While they were walking about aimlessly, someone called, "Peter," from behind. Peter turned his head and found himself in front of an unknown person wearing a railway uniform. The man said, "When did you come back from Mussoori? I am going again to Dehradun. If you want, I can take you." Peter did not understand, but he said, "Yes, I want to go and my friend, Khalifa, also wants to go." The railway man who was the same driver laughed loudly and said, "Okay, I'll take you both. Go and sit in the luggage compartment behind the engine. If anyone asks, tell them you are the driver's people."

The driver was in a hurry to get his papers from the office, so he left and Peter and Khalifa went to the luggage compartment. The driver totally forgot about Peter. When he arrived in Dehradun, he again saw Peter and at once went to him and said, "I forgot about you. Why didn't you come to talk to me in the engine? You could have sat in the engine as you did before." Peter did not understand about his sitting in the engine before. "Maybe he is mistaking me for someone else who might have gone with him before," he thought. Peter tried hard to remember if he had met this man before, but he could not remember him at all. Then he thought that maybe he had seen him in the mission camp. He did not want to tell him that he didn't know him, so Peter said, "Thank you, sir, we arrived comfortably." The driver said, "Are you going to Mussoori?" Peter said, "Yes, sir. We don't have any money. Probably we will get some work in Dehradun to make money, or we will go on by foot." The driver gave Peter twenty rupees, enough for their tickets and food, and said, "Peter you cured my arm and I can't forget you. Go to my parents and tell them I'll visit them next week."

Peter and Khalifa left very happily. They had twenty rupees for the first time after their release from the prison. Khalifa said, "Let's go to the bus station now," and they began to walk into town. On the way, Khalifa said, "Peter, we have money. We can stay here for a day or two and look at the town, and then we can go half way on the bus and walk the rest of the way on foot. It's not very far to walk to Mussoori."

Peter guessed what Khalifa really meant, so they stayed in Dehradun and wandered all around. In the evening, Khalifa said, "Peter, one puff of chandu will take away all the cold from our bones and we can rest for the whole night." Peter was already prepared for it. It was not difficult for them to find a chandu den—chandu smokers can smell out chandu dens just as a jackal can pick up the scent of a dead animal far away in the jungle. They happily smoked chandu and slept, unconscious of the world, for the whole night. The next morning they left for the bus stand, but they were unsure if they really wanted to go to Mussoori.

In the Bareilly child care center, Dorothy somehow heard that some crazy European doctor was living in Mussoori. She thought that he might be her husband, so she decided to go there and try to find her husband and bring him back to Bareilly.

A week later, she took a train to Dehradun and from there, a bus to Mussoori. By chance, the railway driver was in the same bus. He was an Indian Christian. The driver saw a cross hanging on Dorothy's neck and thought she must be some spiritual lady. So he introduced himself by the name of Manik George. He told her that he was a railroad engineer and that his parents were living in Mussoori; he was going to visit them for a month. He said that the winters in Mussoori are very peaceful because very few people stay there due to the cold. Dorothy told about her hope of finding her husband who had disappeared a few months before. They talked on different subjects and became good friends. While their bus was entering the limits of Mussoori, the railway driver, Manik George, saw Peter and Khalifa walking on the footpath, which was a short-cut to Mussoori town. He wanted to stop and talk to them, but they both disappeared behind the hills.

In Mussoori, Dorothy had no place to stay except a hotel. When she asked a coolie to take her to a hotel, Manik George said that she could stay at his parents' house if she wanted. Dorothy thought that it would be nice to stay with his parents, and perhaps he could help her find her husband.

It was winter and there were no clouds in the sky. For several days the weather was pretty warm. It was quite unusual for Mussoori. Manik George and Dorothy enjoyed the beautiful weather of Mussoori. They looked in different places and one day, they heard about the crazy doctor. Dorothy and Manik George went to his place to visit him. They went into the doctor's room and, sure enough, it was Dr. Hey. Dorothy hugged him tightly with tears in her eyes. She said, "Why did you leave Bareilly? Due to your absence the whole hospital work was stopped, and now we have a child care center. It's progressing well." The doctor did not show any concern about the mission or the child care center. He simply said, "It's good that you are serving the poor."

Dorothy introduced Manik George to her husband. They both talked a little and then Manik George thought it would be good if they were left alone to talk openly, so he left.

Peter and Khalifa also reached Mussoori, and Khalifa knew that it would be easy to get a place to sleep in the sweeper community. He was from the sweeper caste and could relate to them very easily. They went to the colony and stayed with an old man who was living alone and needed some help making the fire in his room, collecting wood and hauling water.

All of a sudden, the weather took a turn and the sky was filled with dark clouds. It began to rain heavily. It rained or snowed for two or three days continuously. On Christmas morning people saw the whole mountain covered with four or five feet of snow. All the roads were closed. All the people were shut up in their rooms. After the heavy snowfall, the weather again changed; the sun began to shine and the snow began to melt. In two days there remained only six inches of snow on the roofs, but in shady places it was still the same. People shoveled away the snow from the streets and began going out.

In the sweeper colony, the roof of Bhagatji's room had caved in. The whole box was filled with snow and no one had noticed it. All the sweepers were busy opening the market road and their own footpaths. When the snow was all cleared and people began to walk freely, someone in the colony noticed that the roof of the chicken coop had caved in. Immediately all the people from the colony collected there, and in no time the news spread all over Mussoori that Bhagatji was buried in his own room by the snow. People gathered there and the police came to make a proper inquiry. They started digging the snow out.

Someone said, "Bhagatji can't die. When he can give life to a dead person, how can he die?" Someone else said, "Maybe he left the place before it caved in, and Bhagatji is not buried there." People began to imagine different things until the hand of Bhagatji appeared above the snow. Now there was no doubt that Bhagatji was buried, but still people were thinking that possibly he was still alive. Very slowly the snow was shoveled out and the body of Bhagatji was taken out of the room.

The doctor from the local hospital was not there that day. He had gone to Dehradun and his car was stuck in the snow. The police wanted a doctor to check the body before it was given for its last ceremony. People of all religions—Hindu, Moslem, Christians, rich and poor, everyone was there and everyone was filled with sorrow to see the death of such a high being. Someone suggested the crazy foreign doctor and immediately people went to his room and said, "Bhagatji is dead. The police want a doctor to check the body before it is given for burial." The doctor, Dorothy and Manik George were together talking about spirituality. When the doctor heard about Bhagatji's death, he immediately stood up and went to see him. Dorothy and Manik George followed him.

When they reached the chicken coop, all three were shocked and said, "He is Peter!" The doctor could not stop his tears and began to cry like a child. He said, "Peter, you were beyond religions, a true devotee of God and a real server of mankind. You are my teacher and you opened my eyes." Manik George said, "He cured my arm. A few days ago I brought him to Dehradun in my train. He was really a high soul."

Khalifa and Peter also heard the news and they went to see how a man had died from the snowfall. Khalifa saw the face of Bhagatji and said, "Jhabban!" and then he looked at his friend Peter's face and was confused. Dr. Hey and Dorothy and Manik George also saw Khalifa and Peter. They did not understand which Peter had died, the real Peter or Jhabban. Manik George was surprised to see Peter alive, but he did not know if the dead man had cured his arm or this Peter. They were identical.

The doctor declared him dead and the police searched the clothes of Bhagatji. In the pocket of his old shirt, they found a paper written.

This body will die in Mussoori by burial under the snow on Christmas day. This is the will of God. —Jhabban, Ratlam Hospital, Bareilly District.

Dr. Hey said, "Oh it is truly Jhabban!" and again began to cry. Now Khalifa realized that his real friend was dead and he also began to cry. Until this time, his friend Peter had been Jhabban to him.

When the people who were saying, "He can't die. He is all powerful," saw that Bhagatji was dead, they began to say, "It was only our misguided belief that he gave life to a dead person, healed people and had powers." But when they read the paper written a year before describing his own death, they began to say, "Bhagatji was a real saint. He really foresaw his death."

People of all castes, all religions, the rich and the poor, arranged a procession. They decorated the dead body with flowers and took it to Haridwar. There they dropped it into the River Ganga.

Dr. Hey said, "Jhabban's body served human beings while alive and this body will serve the fish in the water after his death."

No monuments, no temples or churches were made in the name of Jhabban, but all who had ever seen him made a temple to him in their hearts.

Dr. Hey did not go back to Bareilly with his wife. Instead he followed the path of Jhabban, and began to sweep churches, temples, mosques and streets and became a true disciple of Saint Jhabban.

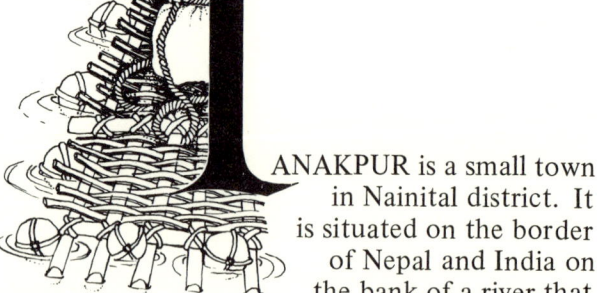ANAKPUR is a small town in Nainital district. It is situated on the border of Nepal and India on the bank of a river that separates the two countries and makes a borderline.

This town is a business place. A special market opens once a week where country people bring their grains, goats, cows and horses to sell, using the money to purchase cloth, salt, oil, etc. for their own use.

On the other side of the river, the villagers of Nepal are very poor. They breed cows and make a purified butter which is called ghee. They come to Tanakpur to sell this ghee.

People of both sides make rafts out of a few poles tied with dry gourds all around, and they cross the river carrying their things on these rafts.

During monsoons the river swells up and is impossible to cross by this kind of raft. So the Nepal villagers store ghee in big cans for three months, and when the rain stops they bring the cans to sell in Tanakpur. So Tanakpur is the big trading place for Nepal ghee.

The Indian merchants purchase the ghee and put it in fancy bottles, tins and jars with beautiful labels and trademarks. Then they sell it for four or five times more than what they paid for it.

These merchants cheat the poor people in different ways—by loaning money at high interest rates and by supplying overpriced cloth and salt. But sometimes the villagers also cheat the merchants. They use a root which becomes like ghee if boiled, and when it is mixed half and half, there is no one who can tell that it is impure until it is heated.

Nepal is full of pine trees; because there are few roads to transport the logs, it is easy and cheap to drift them down the river. So the timber contractors of both India and Nepal use the river to transport the timber, and then they store it in Tanakpur. This business makes Tanakpur a marketplace where merchants purchase timber and then supply it to various other cities by train.

Tanakpur is also a big center for one special kind of business. Thirty years ago this business was quite open and nobody knew that it was illegal. This special business is smuggling things from one side to the other side. The main article of smuggling is hashish.

All of a sudden the Indian government tightened the smuggling of hashish from Nepal to India. It shocked several people at first, because they never knew that smuggling of hashish was illegal.

Moti was a businessman of the third type, although he started as the second type. He was born in Tanakpur. His father was an expert in drifting logs. One day he was hit by a drifting log which crushed his head and he died. Moti was only six years old then. Probably his mother had left with another man when he was younger.

All the laborers who work on drifting wood live together as one family and move from place to place together, so Moti, although he had lost his parents, never felt that he had lost them because he was still living in the same way.

Drifting logs is fun. You have to jump from one log to another to separate the ends of those logs which collect together and stop the flow of water in the right direction. Sometimes it is very dangerous, too.

Moti did not like this work. He preferred to serve people by making chillum (tobacco pipe) for them, to cook food and wash dishes, and to sleep.

Banshi was his friend—a year older than he was and smarter and more energetic. He was very adventurous. Sometimes he would take Moti with him into the deep forest and show him the mountain bear, which is a very dangerous animal. He would make noises to tease the bear and before the bear would attack he would run away dragging Moti with him.

Once they both were on the Nepal side when they met a man who wanted them to carry two bags to the other side of the river. Banshi and Moti prepared their small raft and crossed the river with the two bags. The man was already standing there waiting for them when they arrived. He became very happy and gave them one rupee each. In those days, one rupee was a big amount.

Moti said, "Why did he give us so much money, Banshi? Did you see what was in the bags?" Banshi said, "There was hashish in the bags. I think he sells hashish to people and makes money that way."

Moti said, "Banshi, we have two rupees. We can do the same thing. We don't have to pay carriage charges to anyone either, because we can carry the hashish by ourselves."

Banshi agreed to the idea and from that day on, they became hashish smugglers. It was a very easy job. They earned much money.

On the Indian side of the river, there was an old temple that had been deserted for several years. So Moti and Banshi made this temple into their storeroom.

Wealth doesn't come alone. When it comes, it comes with its friend—greed. For several years Moti and Banshi worked together. They started a gambling booth and prostitution, and they also began to drink alcohol. The more they earned, the more they spent.

Moti used to live on the Nepal side. He would collect hashish and bring it to the temple from where Banshi would sell it to others. So Banshi was known to everyone in Tanakpur as a hashish seller, but nobody knew about Moti.

In the Nepal villages, people make alcohol out of rice and barley, which is very strong and cheap, and very addicting. Moti used to drink it all the time and he became an alcoholic. The strong alcohol damaged his mind. He stopped shaving his beard, cutting his hair and taking a bath. Sometimes he would forget to wear clothes.

One day while he was drunk he crossed the river, wrapping a blanket around himself. When he reached a place near the temple, he saw that Banshi was handcuffed and being taken away by the police. Banshi also saw Moti but pretended that he didn't know him, so that the police would not arrest him too.

Moti went into the temple. There was nothing there. He sat down in one corner watching the walls, unconcerned. Smuggling of goods was completely stopped. Several people were arrested and it was difficult to cross the river now because of rains. Moti's business was finished, but his desire for alcohol had increased. He was only forty years old, but his face was all wrinkled; with his gray beard, long gray hair and skinny, tall body, he appeared as if he were seventy-five years old. All the time his eyes were looking for alcohol. His tongue was thirsty for one drop of alcohol. But he had no money and no hashish to sell, so there was nothing to do. He spread his blanket on the floor and sat nude over it.

There is an old, famous temple in Tanakpur on the top of a high mountain. Every year devotees of different parts of India come to visit this temple, and Tantra Yoga practitioners sit on the top of the mountain and chant sacred mantras. One of these devotees, who went to take a bath in the river, saw Moti's deserted temple and, out of curiosity, went in. He found a hermit with long, gray beard and hair sitting nude on the floor. He at once guessed that he might be a Tantric yogi. He bowed to him with much reverence but the old man remained sitting unconcerned. This influenced the man very much and he left at once for the market where he purchased two bottles of alcohol, fruit and a few other things; then he went back to the temple and offered the gifts to the old man.

The old man recognized the bottles and immediately drank one bottle all at once. It surprised the devotee very much. He thought that the old man must be some high being, so he bowed to him several times and returned to the place where he was staying.

He was very happy that he had found a real yogi. He told

his friends that a "Malang Sahib" (a very high saint for whom good and bad makes no difference) was living in the temple. Slowly people began to visit Malang Sahib every day. Everyone knew that he didn't want anything except alcohol. So the devotees would take alcohol to him every day, and they began to feed him and clean the place.

Nobody knew that his name was Moti. Everyone called him Malang Sahib. He was illiterate. He had never lived with any other hermits and he had not learned any spiritual practices. It was only his long, gray beard and hair and his sitting nude and unconcerned that made him Malang Sahib. No one saw him angry or happy. He never asked anyone to do anything for him. All these things attracted people and they believed that he was a Malang Sahib.

If people asked a question, he would not reply. Sometimes, a new person would ask him why he drank so much and one of his devotees would reply, "Oh, for him it is no different if he drinks alcohol or the sacred water of the Ganga. Don't you see he is sitting among us, but he is really not here. Maybe he's somewhere in the astral plane."

A businessman visited the Goddess Temple and prayed for an hour to get rid of his sins and to collect virtues, and then he returned to the place where he was staying. He had heard about the mysterious Malang Sahib and wanted to see him. He put two bottles of wine, fruits, tea and sugar in a basket. Finding Malang Sahib in the deserted temple, he bowed to him with much reverence and offered the basket.

The devotees told him about the high stage of Malang Sahib and how he could drink alcohol, one bottle at a time, how he sat in the same mood all of the time. The businessman was much impressed and prayed, "Sir, if I get some kind of business in Tanakpur, by your grace, then I'll rebuild this temple. It is only by your blessing that I can get some work."

After waiting for a while, the businessman left for his own place.

It was the end of the rainy season. The villagers from Nepal came with ghee earlier than usual because the rain had stopped early. The regular purchasers of ghee had not yet arrived. The businessman of Kanpur, seeing so much ghee, purchased all of it at a good price and supplied it to his Kanpur contacts. He made good connections with the small ghee contractors to supply him with ghee whenever it was needed.

Due to less rain, food prices at once soared and the big stockholders began to hold onto all of the stocks. This increased prices several times more.

The businessman of Kanpur earned lots of money by holding the stock of ghee for two years. He realized that it was all due to the grace of Malang Sahib. He remembered his word, also, to rebuild the temple. Sometimes he would think that he had made the profit due to his fate and so he really didn't need to spend money in rebuilding the temple. Other times he would think that if he didn't fulfill his word, then probably Malang Sahib would curse him. So he decided to go to Tanakpur and pay his respect to Malang Sahib.

MALANG SAHIB was now well known in Tanakpur. Tanakpur was developing very fast because of its business situation. The number of devotees of Malang Sahib was also developing day by day. When the Kanpur businessman reached the temple, he found several people sitting there. He bowed to Malang Sahib by laying flat on the ground and said, "Sir, by your grace, I have earned much money in the business of ghee. As I promised in front of you to rebuild this temple, I'll do it now. Sir, I have a good market for ghee and I want to use your picture on the labels of my cans and bottles. The labels will read, 'Malang Sahib Ghee'."

There was no one to answer, but it was presumed that Malang Sahib had given his permission in front of so many people, because he did not say "no".

The photographer took several pictures of Malang Sahib to pick out the most suitable one. Within a month, there were advertisements all over with a picture of Malang Sahib. There were also pamphlets on the roadsides with his pictures advertising ghee.

Now businessmen, gamblers and others who wanted to make money began to visit Malang Sahib to get his blessing. Some earned money and some lost. Those who earned money made up several stories about Malang Sahib's powers and those who lost remained silent and blamed their own fate.

In two years, the new temple with a special room for Malang Sahib and a room for his devotees was completed. The devotees started to worship in both the morning and the evening. Every Saturday, all night chanting of mantras was also started. The temple, which had been deserted for so long and which was used for smuggling, gambling and prostitution by Moti and Banshi, was now a very spiritual place.

On one auspicious day, a new deity of the goddess Kali was seated there. The public arranged to take out a procession of the deity all over the town before giving her a permanent seat in the temple. Two palanquins were prepared, one for the deity Kali and one for Malang Sahib. With much pomp and show and with different kinds of musical instruments and chanting of sacred words, the procession was taken on every street of Tanakpur. Devotees threw offerings of flowers onto both palanquins and women tossed garlands from their rooftops.

It was a huge procession. When it passed through the railway station, Banshi was just coming out of the station after completing four years of imprisonment in Bareilly Jail. He was very weak and hardly able to walk. He saw the procession pass and hurried to see what was happening. When he saw Moti sitting on the palanquin covered with flowers and completely drunk, as always, Banshi cried, "Moti! Moti! You stupid! I was jailed for four years and here you are being worshiped as a king!" His jealousy burst out. He shouted, "He is not a saint. He is a fake. He was a smuggler. He was a gambler. He was my partner in all crimes."

Some devotees heard him abusing Malang Sahib and they angrily said, "Shut up, you crazy!" One young man went up to Banshi and slapped him on his face. Banshi was very weak. One slap was enough. He began to see stars inside his head and fell down on his knees for a few minutes.

The procession moved on at its own speed. The devotees were chanting *Jai Ma Kali Jai Ma Durga* with much emotion. Some were dancing. Some were blowing conch shells and ringing bells. When Banshi came to his senses, he also started singing and dancing with the people.

The procession reached the temple and the deity Kali was given a seat in her proper place after all the rites and rituals were performed.

Malang Sahib was given a seat in his new room, but he was so drunk that he was unable to move his body. Everyone still wanted him to accept their offerings of alcohol. When everything had been performed peacefully, the devotees went to bow to Malang Sahib, but they found he was dead!

Banshi was among the crowd, still afraid of the people because that one slap had opened his brain. When he heard that Malang Sahib was dead, he laughed loudly and then he remembered the slap, so he stopped laughing and said in a low voice, "Some people strive to become famous; some become famous by their talents; and at some people fame *throws* herself."

Banshi joined the burial ceremony of his only friend, Moti. Everyone left after giving the grave to Malang Sahib. But Banshi remained sitting there all night, passing through the pain of attachment, jealousy and anger.

Malang Sahib is not in this world, but the "Malang Sahib Ghee" is spreading his fame everywhere. The devotees now believe that he was capable of flying in the sky and walking on the ocean. Only Banshi knows the truth. But he still remembers the slap, so he also chants the same songs as the other devotees.

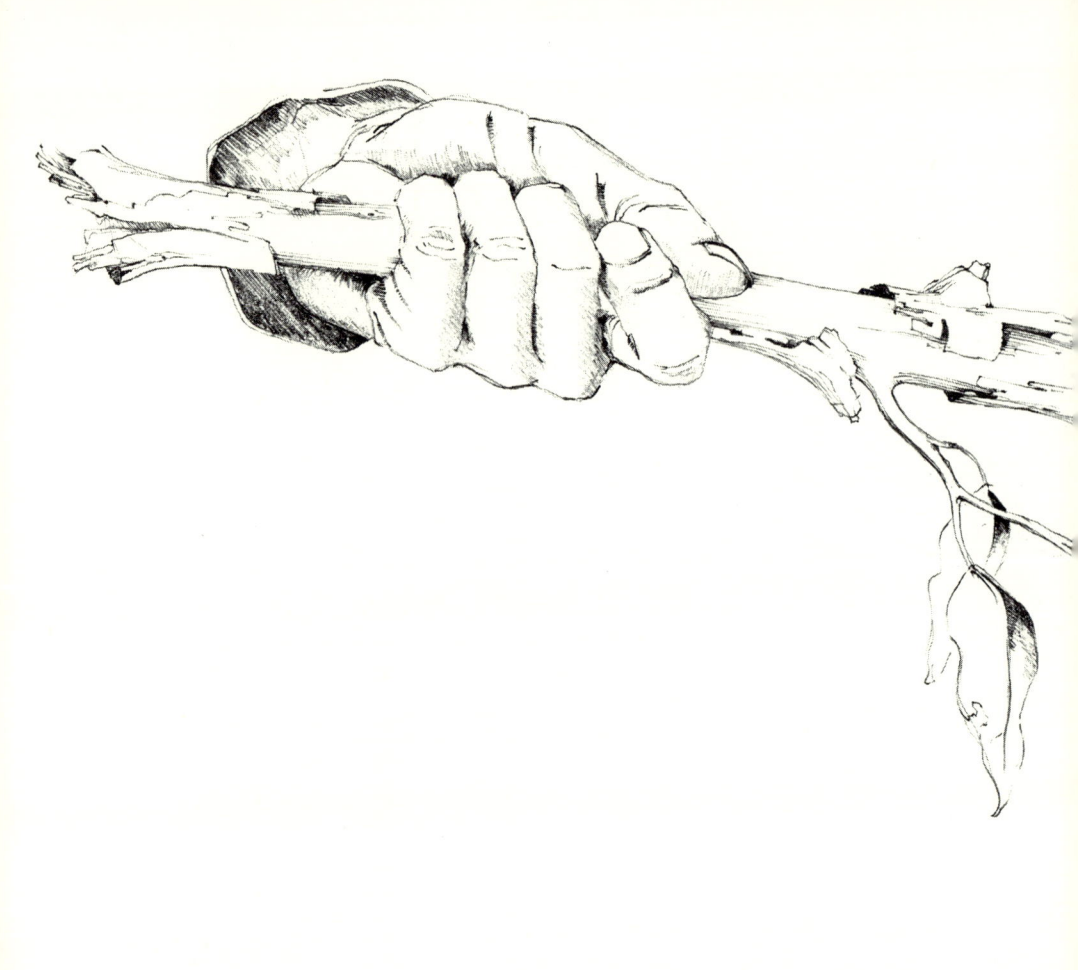

Blind Poet

NO ONE knows how it is that someone is born with an extraordinary talent for music, art, poetry, mathematics, or physics. But from time to time such people are born. In a small village near Dehradun, Chintu was born a poet. His parents, Debram and Champo, were very poor.

Just before Chintu's birth, Debram went to the next village to bring back some friends because Champo was having a difficult labor. While he was gone Chintu was born, but his mother did not survive the birth. When Debram came back with a few neighbors, he found a beautiful baby crying by the side of his wife. Debram said, "Champo, how are you?" A neighbor woman bent over her and said, "She is all blue—maybe she is dead!"

An old man of the village came and checked Champo's pulses. He said, "Yes, she is dead." When Debram heard his wife was dead, he felt as if the ground below his feet were sinking. He sat down holding his head. After a while he cried very loudly saying, "My wife is dead. Who will take care of this child? Who will cook food for me? I am a poor man. I have no money to get another woman. Oh, I am ruined!" The neighbors consoled him by saying that they would take care of his child, that if he made some money in the future he could marry another woman.

No one dies to keep the dead company. The world goes on at its own speed. Debram started his work of skinning dead animals. He sold the hide, horns and bones to contractors, but he got very little money. Also several days would go by when he could not find any dead animal; then he would either starve or borrow food from the neighbors.

Chintu was taken in by an old woman who had no children or relatives left at home. She had some land which brought her enough food for the whole year. Debram no longer had to worry about his child, but a new worry came into his head and that was to get a wife. It was impossible for him to make money if he didn't find enough dead animals to skin. The villagers had cows, goats and horses, but they were generally healthy. Sometimes one or two old animals died and Debram got the hide and horns; sometimes he found dead animals in distant villages too. Debram said to himself, "If God sends some kind of disease and the animals start dying every day, then I can be rich." All of a sudden his eyes enlarged and his face glowed with an inner smile as if some solution had been found.

He went to the jungle with a pickaxe and an empty sack. Climbing high up on the mountains, he dug up a kind of root; it was somewhat like onion, but very small. He collected one bagful of the root and came home.

The next morning a villager came to Debram and said that his cow had died during the night and he wanted to have it removed. Debram would get the hide and horns in payment for removing the corpse from the village.

Debram said, "What happened to your cow? Yesterday I saw your cow and it was perfectly all right. Maybe some disease is spreading among the animals."

The next day another man's cow died, and then several more died. Debram's yard was filled with hides and horns. He was very busy skinning the corpses every day.

The head man of the village went to the animal doctor and told him about the unknown disease. The doctor said he would inspect the animals. The next day when the doctor went to the village, the head man's beautiful horse was dying. The doctor checked the dying horse and checked the grass the horse had eaten. He asked if all the animals had died in the same way. The villagers said yes, they had never shown any symptoms of sickness. The doctor picked up a root from the grass and said, "This is poisonous for animals. How did it get here?" The head man said, "Last night I put grass out for my horse by myself and I know it was not there then. Now I remember, Debram came early this morning and asked if my horse was sick. I told him to go and see if the horse was all right. No one else came to my stable."

The horse died and Debram was called to remove the corpse. Debram came and said, "Sir, I saw the horse in the morning. I found him a little sad and sleepy. I think there is some dangerous disease. What did the doctor say?" The head man said, "The doctor still doesn't know if it is a disease or poison." Debram went to remove the horse.

On his way home the doctor thought he should go and see Debram's place where all the hides were kept. Without telling anybody, the doctor went to Debram's hut and found the poisonous root in a sack. He went home and informed the police.

After he skinned the horse Debram went home. The hide and horn contractor was sitting there. Debram said, "Did you bring enough money to buy all this?" The contractor smiled and said, "Don't you trust me? If there is any shortage of money I will pay later on." After bargaining for the whole lot of hide and horns the price was settled at 110 rupees. The contractor said, "Debram, don't worry, I'll pay 110 rupees right now. I can see you don't trust me." Debram laughed and said, "I trust you. You know I want the money because I am just about to get married."

At that very moment the police arrived and said, "Debram, a woman is ready to marry you. Let's go." They handcuffed him and took the sack of roots with them. Debram was married to the walls of the jail.

In the old woman's house, Chintu began to grow. He was very smart, playful and healthy, but he was not lucky. No one can have everything. Chintu had everything but good luck: the kind old woman died when he was just two years old. He could walk and talk but people in the village were unwilling to take Chintu into their homes because he was considered a bad omen. They said, "As soon as he stepped on the earth his mother died. After three months his father went to jail, and after two years the old lady died."

The head man of the village took Chintu to an orphanage in Dehradun town, where he began to live with other children. Most of the children in the orphanage were either lazy, dumb or ugly, but Chintu was the opposite. He was very beautiful, very smart and very energetic. The woman who owned the orphanage fell in love with Chintu; instead of keeping him in the orphanage, she kept him in her own house, which was a few blocks away.

She started teaching Chintu how to read and write when he was only three years old, and when he was four he began to make poems. The woman was astonished at his marvellous mind. But all of a sudden when Chintu was six years old an illness left him blind. A kind of cloud covered both eyes and he could not see a thing. Chintu was not worried about it but the woman became very sad because the doctors said that they didn't have any cure for this kind of blindness.

Chintu started singing poems and whenever the woman heard him singing she wrote down the poems. After she had collected several of his poems, she thought about getting them published. But thinking that he would sing even better poems when he was older, she decided to wait. After a few years, when Chintu was thirteen, the woman needed money. She sold the poems to a publisher and got enough money to take good care of him.

THE WOMAN had a niece named Bhavani, who was the same age as Chintu. She would come to play with Chintu. Although Chintu was blind, his desire to play was strong. Sometimes they would play "blindman's bluff"; sometimes they would go out for a walk. Bhavani's aunt was very happy to see them playing together and told her that whenever Chintu sang a poem to write it down in a notebook.

Bhavani heard from her aunt that Chintu's father was in prison, but she was told never to talk to Chintu about his father or mother. The woman did not want Chintu to feel that he was not her son. Once she took Bhavani to a garden where prisoners were sowing vegetables. Debram was also working there. Bhavani's aunt said, "Look, that is Chintu's father. After the death of Chintu's mother he wanted to marry, but he was very poor so he poisoned the village cows to get money from selling their hides and horns. The police arrested him and now he is jailed." Bhavani said, "He seems to be a good man. Look how he is making jokes and laughing."

Chintu and Bhavani became so close that her aunt decided to get them married, although they both were only nineteen years old.

Bhavani's aunt had taken care of Chintu for seventeen years, and now she was very old. Because of Chintu's poems she took in lots of money, built a new house and made the orphanage bigger. But she also died one day due to old age. Chintu's seventeen years' association with her finished. He became very sad and began to feel as if the house, the people, the whole town were trying to swallow him.

He said, "Bhavani, take me to some secluded place where I'll not hear the sound of people, where no one but you will meet me. I want to live with deer, birds and trees. This place is biting me." Bhavani felt his pain and realized if he were not removed from here, he probably would go crazy. She sold the house and other things and they moved to the mountains, to a small village in Mussoori.

Chintu's father had poisoned so many cattle; it was a big crime for which he served ten years in jail. When he was released he was no longer interested in marriage and earning money. He left for a holy place with the thought to become a monk—he believed that by becoming a monk his sins would wash away. So when he reached Haridwar he became a monk and lived in a temple. He almost forgot that he had a son.

Chintu was now very happy living in the mountains. Poems began to flow out of him; the singing of birds and the whistling sound of pine trees opened his heart and he sang and danced in bliss.

In a small town everyone knows everyone. When Chintu and Bhavani came to Mussoori they knew no one, but gradually people became friendly. When they discovered that Chintu was a great poet they started visiting him. A young man in the town, named Ravi Shankar, was a story writer. He was very fond of Chintu's poems and had read several of his books. When he heard that Chintu was living near the same town, he went to visit him. Chintu and Ravi Shankar became good friends because both had similar taste in writing.

Ravi Shankar would visit Chintu's place every day and stay there for hours. Chintu was very happy at finding a friend who loved his poems. Ravi Shankar not only loved his poems, he also began to love Bhavani. Bhavani was attracted to Ravi Shankar because he could see how beautiful she was—a woman always wants a man to appreciate her beauty. Chintu could only appreciate her beauty in an abstract way, because he was blind. Bhavani felt that there was something missing in Chintu's love for her. She said to herself, "He can't see me. How can he appreciate my beauty? How can he love me? He is a poet and in his mind I am a poem. He only sings poems about how beautiful I am. He doesn't really feel it." She began to feel love for Ravi Shankar, who was a handsome young man. Ravi Shankar started taking advantage of Chintu's blindness. He and Bhavani would sit together and enjoy their youth.

Once Bhavani went out with Ravi Shankar for a short walk. Ravi Shankar expressed his feelings and asked if she is ready to live with him. By now Bhavani was deeply in love with Ravi Shankar, but she was afraid to leave Chintu all alone in the darkness of his blindness. She said, "I am afraid, Ravi Shankar—I can't leave him as long as he is alive." Busy talking, Ravi Shankar stepped on a black cobra snake. He screamed with fear and jumped away. When he looked closely he saw it was a dead snake. He whispered something in Bhavani's ear and, taking the snake on a stick, they went home.

Bhavani went to her house and very politely said, "My dear,

I am late. I bought some fish. You have not eaten fish for a long time. I'll cook it." She cut the snake in pieces and fried it in a pan and went to Chintu's room. She said, "Dear, I have to go to meet my younger sister for an hour. Ravi Shankar can take me and bring me back. You have nothing to do except to put one cup of water in the pan after fifteen minutes. It will be ready in ten minutes after that. Don't wait for me. I'll be at my sister's place."

Chintu said, "Yes, I can do that. Don't worry. You can stay with your sister as long as you want." While they were talking, Bhavani collected all the manuscripts of poems and she and Ravi Shankar left, taking all the poems.

After fifteen minutes Chintu opened the lid of the pot and all the steam gushed into his eyes. He at once put the cup of water in and covered the pan with its lid. Both his eyes began to burn. He rubbed them and rinsed them in cold water, but it did not help. But he was very hungry and it had been a long time since he had had fish, so he was very eager to eat. Although his eyes were still burning, he again went to the kitchen and opened the lid to find out if the fish was cooked. Again the steam gushed into his eyes and he fainted. When he came to his senses the food was burnt and the room was filled with smoke. He took the pan off of the stove and put water in it. Again the room was filled with steam.

Chintu could not tolerate the burning sensation in his eyes, so he went to his room and lay down on his bed. For the whole night he was in an intoxicated state of mind and did not know anything about the time or place he was in.

In the morning he came to his senses and rubbed his eyes. While he was rubbing his eyes he suddenly became aware that he could see his hands. Then he looked around the room and was very surprised that he could see everything. He became very happy and ran out of his room saying, "Bhavani, I can see! Bhavani, I can see!" But there was no answer.

He said, "Oh, I remember—she went to see her sister for one hour with Ravi Shankar. She will be back soon. When she learns that I can see, she will be very happy. I'll clean up the pan and kitchen so that she can sit with me uninterrupted." He went to the kitchen and saw some pieces of food half burnt in the pan. "What is this? Is it a fish? No, it seems to be something else." He put the pan aside to check with Bhavani and then cleaned the kitchen. An hour passed, then two hours, and then night came, but Bhavani did not return. Chintu waited for the whole night for her and in the morning he fell asleep. When he woke up it was noon. He came out of the house and ran down the road screaming, "Bhavani! Bhavani!" A monk was strolling on the roadside and he saw Chintu running and screaming like a crazy. The monk went to him and asked, "What's the matter?" Chintu said, "My wife left me. She did not come home. Where is she?"

The monk laughed and said, "My wife also left me when I was young, but not intentionally. She died in giving birth to a child."

The monk quoted a verse in Sanskrit which meant, "Pen, book and wife—once they go to another's hand they never come back." "Young man, don't worry about it. Earn money and marry another woman. What do you do?"

Chintu said, "I am a poet, I have several books ready to publish. But I want Bhavani, I don't want anyone else. I want to see her face. For so long I was blind and she lived with me; now that my eyes are opened, she has left me." His tears began to fall.

The monk said, "Let's go to your house. Perhaps I can find some clue to her whereabouts." They both went home and Chintu said, "She asked me to cook the fish and eat it. 'Don't wait for me. I am visiting my sister,' she said." The monk saw the pan and said, "Do you call this fish? Young man, you are crazy. It is poisonous snake. Did you eat it?" Chintu said, "No. But when I was cooking it, steam gushed up in my eyes. It burned my eyes and I fainted. I think the steam of this poison cured my blindness."

Chintu looked for his manuscripts but found nothing. He said, "Oh, everything is gone." He began to laugh. "God is merciful. When I was blind he gave me a wife, and when my wife left He gave me eyes." The monk also laughed and said, "Really, God is merciful. When my wife died he made me a prisoner, and when I was released from prison, he made me a beggar." They both began to laugh.

Chintu said, "Sir, why don't you live with me. I can earn money easily and you don't have to beg food. Live with me." The monk said, "All right. A saint and a snake don't make their nests. They use the nests of others. I'll live with you as long as it is comfortable."

BHAVANI & Ravi Shankar immediately left the town and began to live in Allahabad—a place of intellectuals, artists, and poets. Ravi Shankar got Chintu's poems published under his name and got a lot of money. For some time they lived happily, but Ravi Shankar was a gambler. He would gamble every day. At first Bhavani did not know that he gambled; she thought he went out to some club for writers or that he had some kind of job. But then he began to come home drunk and quarrelsome. He would fight with Bhavani if she told him not to drink and come home late at night.

Ravi Shankar lost all the money he got from Chintu's poems. His stories were not worth publishing and he had no skill at doing anything. It was difficult for him to feed himself, and with Bhavani he had to earn money to feed two people. He began to live on the streets or near the bank of the River Ganga. Sometimes he would come home and steal Bhavani's clothes or ornaments to sell in the market. Bhavani had kept a few manuscripts hidden in which Chintu sang of her beauty and how he felt for her. They were unique poems, filled with abstract images which the imagination of an average person could scarcely grasp. She had not allowed those poems to be published, because they were her most valuable possession. They were her love and her life. When she saw that Ravi Shankar had stolen all her clothes and ornaments, she was afraid that he would steal the manuscripts, so she decided to run away from him.

That same night Ravi Shankar came home totally drunk and asked her to give him money. When Bhavani said that she had no money, he went mad and started beating her. He beat her so mercilessly that she fainted. Ravi Shankar took off all her clothes and left. When Bhavani came to her senses she found herself nude. She still had one old sari that she wore while cooking food. She at once covered herself with that old sari. She thought that if he came again he would kill her, so she took the manuscripts, which she had hidden under the floor, and took the train for Dehradun, where her parents lived in one corner of the town. Bhavani was positive that Chintu was no longer in the world. She knew that Chintu loved to eat fish and that if he ate even a little poisonous snake he would die. So she had no thought of Chintu, but she wanted to go to Mussoori to get her clothes she had left in the house. However, she needed money, so she decided to get the last manuscripts published. She went to the publisher who first published Chintu's books and told him that Chintu was dead and the money from the books should be given to her.

Chintu and the monk were very happy together. The monk was old and had no responsibilities, so he was a very humorous and happy person. Chintu also had no worries, but Bhavani was still deep in his mind. However he kept himself happy and tried not to show his pain.

Once Chintu said, "Sir, let's go to Dehradun. I'll show you the place where I was brought up. I want to see it because I was blind then and I don't know what it looks like. Also, I have to get my books published now." The monk was ready to go anywhere. He said, "Well, if you want to show me your place, then I'll show you the place where I was brought up. Probably you will not like me if you see my place. But I don't care. The past is passed, the future is unknown and in the present I am a monk, happy and contented."

They went to Dehradun, which is not very far from Mussoori Mountain. The people in the orphanage and others who had known Chintu for several years could not believe that his eyes could be cured—he had been totally blind. He recognized people by their voices and called them by name when they talked to him. So people accepted that he really was Chintu.

Chintu took the manuscripts and went to the publisher on the very same day that Bhavani had gone there. The publisher called both into his office and gave them chairs to sit on. Bhavani looked at Chintu and said to herself, "He is exactly like Chintu. But he has beautiful eyes and Chintu was totally blind. I know Chintu's father. He was in prison. He had no other son." Then she thought that sometimes two faces resemble each other and did not give any importance to her thoughts.

The publisher turned to Bhavani and said, "Let me see the manuscripts." He asked, "Is it all your handwriting?" Bhavani said, "Yes, it is all written in my own handwriting." The publisher read a few pages here and there and said, "Yes, I will publish it." When Chintu heard her voice he said to himself, "Her voice is exactly like Bhavani's. Who knows, maybe she is Bhavani." At the same time the publisher said to him, "Let me see your manuscripts." He read a few pages and said, "It is a marvellous collection of poems. These are the same kind of poems the famous poet, Chintu, once wrote." Chintu said, "I am Chintu. I was blind before, but once my wife cooked a snake; its steam gushed into my eyes and I began to see."

The publisher said, "This lady says Chintu is dead and she is his wife, Bhavani. She wants his poems to be published. I don't know who you are."

As soon as Chintu heard that she was Bhavani, he jumped from his seat and fell in Bhavani's lap. He cried and cried and said, "Bhavani, why did you leave me? With you I was happy as a blind; without you my eyes can see the world but they don't show me real love. I found you. I found you. Don't leave me again."

Bhavani was feeling very guilty on the one hand; on the other hand she was feeling real love for Chintu. Her mind began to switch very fast between pleasure and pain. She could not think what to say. She had always had real love for Chintu, but for a short time the desire of sensual pleasure confused her mind and blinded her eyes.

The publisher again said, "Which manuscript is written by the real Chintu?" Bhavani said, "Both." She hugged Chintu with tears in her eyes and said, "Chintu, forget about what I did to you. Forgive me. Accept me. Don't leave me in this world alone."

The publisher said, "Now that you have found each other, I'll publish both manuscripts." He gave a large advance payment to Chintu. Chintu said, "Bhavani, I don't keep money. You always kept the money. Now take this." They both went to the orphanage where Chintu was staying. The monk was there. Chintu said, "Bhavani, we live together at Mussoori." Bhavani looked at the monk deeply and said, "You look like Debram, Chintu's father."

The monk said, "Yes, I was Debram, but I don't know if I am Chintu's father. I remember once my wife gave birth to a child and the child was taken away by people who are now dead."

Bhavani said, "Yes, I know you are Chintu's father. I saw you working in a garden with other prisoners once." When Chintu heard the monk was his father, he and Bhavani both kneeled and bowed to his feet. But when they raised their heads they saw the monk running away very fast.

Chintu said, "He was my father, but he is now beyond worldly relationships. He doesn't want family ties. Bhavani, let's go to Mussoori. We will make our world new again."

Destiny

RAJASTHAN is a province in the center of India. It was the center of brave Rajput kings who fought several battles with foreign powers. Even during the reign of the British, several states of Rajasthan were independent and had their own government, although they were under the sovereignty of British rule.

Rajasthan people are tall, hardy, strong; they are good warriors and horsemen. Their occupation is farming, but due to scanty rainfall the farmers can't grow enough food for all the people. Wheat, maize, barley, gram and millet are the principal crops because they need less water.

The western part of Rajasthan is a desert where there is no water and nothing grows. But the state is rich in mineral resources, like marble and gypsum. So the people are good craftsmen and do different kinds of things like weaving, enameling, pottery, papiermache, embroidery, etc. In this way they earn their livelihood.

Several times in the past Rajasthan was hit by a drought, which killed many people and animals. Rajasthan was also devastated in several wars but those brave Rajputs rebuilt Rajasthan again and again.

It was during the period of British rule in the 1930's when Rajasthan was hit by the worst drought. The rain stopped completely for two or three years. The water which was available in small rivers and wells completely dried up. There was no crop and no grass. The kings who ruled the different states tried their best to arrange food and water for their subjects, but their efforts were in vain. They remained silent and helpless, which caused havoc among the public.

People began to leave their homes, their land and most of their possessions. The old and sick were left behind. Everyone wanted to save his life first. Thousands of people from different parts of Rajasthan were leaving every day. Those who could took trains and buses and reached other provinces, and those who had no means of getting conveyances walked by foot in huge caravans.

Several died on the way and no one took the time to bury their bodies. In the scorching heat of the sun some dead bodies dried out and some were eaten up by the dogs and jackals. Because everyone's life was in danger, no one had sympathy for others. Selfishness increased so much that one could snatch food from a child and eat it.

In one of the caravans there was a six-year-old boy who was following a woman. Everyone thought that the woman had lost her husband and was going with her child to some other place. When the woman walked fast the boy could not keep up with her, and so he began to follow another woman. Sometimes some kind man would give him a ride on his back, thinking the boy was very tired from walking and wouldn't survive if not given some rest.

Because Rajasthan was ruled by different kings, the British government did not bother to supply food to Rajasthan. But they did arrange camps on the borders of Rajasthan where people were put up in tents and given food.

There was fear of cholera or smallpox breaking out, so the British government did not want to let people go to different provinces and spread disease all over the country. In each camp there were doctors, Red Cross workers and Boy Scouts who would check each person before allowing him to go to another province.

The caravan in which the six-year-old boy traveled also arrived at the camp and everyone got a place to rest. They all had to get food from one place, so early in the morning they made a queue. The boy was standing somewhere in the middle, behind a woman. When he reached the table he was not seen by the distributors, so he did not get food. The boy began to cry. A woman in the line saw him crying. She had her husband and two children in the queue. She at once said, "Gopal, what happened? Didn't you get food?" The boy said, "No, I am hungry."

The woman picked him up on her lap and told the distributor that Gopal should get his share. The distributor gave him a full share which was enough for a grown-up man. The woman took her share and brought Gopal to her tent. Gopal was not his real name, but because the woman called him Gopal, which was a name for baby Krishna, everyone began to call him Gopal.

Now Gopal knew a trick. He would go with some woman to get food and ask her to lift him up on her lap. He would give the leftover food to the woman. In this way he stayed with several women and introduced himself by the name of Gopal.

Gopal was from a Rajput family so his body build was strong and he was very handsome. His parents were farmers, but both died from some disease while leaving their village due to the famine. From that time Gopal was following different people.

The caravan in which Gopal was staying was allowed to go to Uttar Pradesh Province (in those days the British called it United Province), which was the most fertile province. People could get jobs there in farms, factories and mills.

The caravan divided into small groups and left for different towns and cities of Uttar Pradesh. Gopal followed a group in which there were old and invalid people. That group decided to go to Banares. Banares is a sacred place for Hindus and it is their belief that if someone dies in Banares he gets salvation. Also Banares is a place where no one can remain hungry; pilgrims from all over India come there and distribute food to the poor. Probably this was the reason that the group of old people chose to go there, and Gopal chose this group because the people were slow, compassionate and caring for others.

Gopal reached Banares with the group. There he found that he was better off by himself. He would get more alms and food from the pilgrims when he was alone. So he left the group and began to live at the main bathing place by the bank of the River Ganga, named Manikarnika Ghat.

Because Banares was the center of knowledge from an unknown period of time, high intellectuals, saints and Sanskrit scholars live there. Because it is a place of salvation, old people live there to die. Because it is a place of austerity to purify the mind and body, widows and aspirants of Yoga come there to do their spiritual practices. Because it is an abode of Lord Shiva whose conveyance is a bull, rich people donate bulls to the main temple and hundreds of bulls roam the streets. Behind all this all kinds of bad people like thieves, pickpockets and cheats also live there very safely. It's a heaven for the beggars, where they get things without asking.

Gopal was getting food from people from the day he left his village so he did not think that begging food was a bad thing. He started standing on the street of the main Shiva Temple, where beggars sit on both sides. All of the pilgrims would give alms to them when going in, and on their return they would give the sweets or other offerings they brought back from the temple. This tradition has been carried on from ages past. Sometimes some rich man would give a blanket to each beggar during winter or a cloth to wear during summer. So the beggars were much better off than the working people.

Gopal was very happy in Banares. After getting alms, food, fruits and sweets in the morning, he would play all day with other boys at the main bathing place.

He noticed that his friends bowed to the people who wore orange robes. Curiously he asked his friends who those people were. His friends said, "They are no ordinary people. They are sannyasins. They are like gods. That's why everyone is supposed to bow to them and obey their orders." Gopal saw lots of orange-robed people coming and going in the temple and he had never bowed to them because he did not know who they were. But now whenever he would see any orange-colored robe he would bow with much reverence. In this way five years passed and Gopal did not change his way of living, although he was big enough to find a job now.

ONCE IN THE MORNING while Gopal was standing on the street corner he saw a tall man with long hair, a beard and a moustache dressed in an orange-colored robe, wearing an orange-colored turban and holding a stick with a silver handle. He was strong, with a broad chest, and his gait was like an elephant's. Gopal bowed to the sannyasin as usual and again stood on the corner. The sannyasin glanced at him and walked to the temple. After getting enough fruits, sweets and loose coins Gopal left the street and went to his place in the main bathing place by the bank of the River Ganga. The tall sannyasin, after coming out of the temple, looked around as if looking for someone and then he proceeded to the main bathing place (Manikarnika Ghat). He found the same boy sitting on a bench facing the river and eating sweets. The sannyasin came in front of him and Gopal again bowed to him with much reverence. The sannyasin sat down on the same bench and said, "You look like you are from Rajasthan." The boy said, "Yes, I came from Rajasthan with a group of people. They are all scattered here and there." The sannyasin said, "Where are your parents?" Gopal said, "I don't have any parents. They died on the way."

The sannyasin said, "Oh, you are all alone, or maybe you are living with your relatives. Where do you live?" Gopal said, "I don't live with anybody. I live by myself. Do you see that corner? There is a large table. I live under that table. In the town it is too hot and there is much noise all the time. Here it is cool at night. I sleep very well here. Also, I have friends here who come to play by the river."

The sannyasin said, "I have a place on the other side of the Ganga. There are lots of boys of your age. There is a river where the boys swim and go in small boats. There are several horses. They take the horses into the jungles for grazing. There are cows and a fruit garden. There are beautiful huts for everyone. Also they sing and dance. Why don't you go with me? You will be very happy there. You will get everything you need."

Gopal had much respect for sannyasins and he had heard from his friends that we should obey sannyasins. He thought if he lived with such a high being he would he happy, and moreover he would be obeying a sannyasin.

Gopal said, "How will you cross the river? It is very deep." The sannyasin smiled and said, "Oh, I have a boat here." He whistled and a boatman raised his oars in the sky. The sannyasin said, "Do you see? That is my boat." Gopal said, "Oh, I know that man. He often comes and talks to me. Yes. I'll go with you."

The sannyasin and Gopal left for the boat. When the boat was in mid-stream the sannyasin said, "Oh, I forgot to ask your name. What is your name?" The boy said, "Gopal." The sannyasin said, "Oh, it's a beautiful name. It's a name of Lord Krishna."

The boat touched the bank and there were two horses waiting for the sannyasin. The sannyasin climbed on a horse and put Gopal on his lap. The man who was waiting rode on the other horse and they both galloped down a dirt road. They crossed several villages and reached a jungle; by the late afternoon they reached a village surrounded by a jungle. It was getting dark and Gopal was tired from the all-day journey, so the sannyasin gave him a room close to his house. After eating food Gopal slept like a dead.

The next morning when he woke up he was very surprised to see himself among very different people. There were children of his age. There were horses and there was a garden and a river. Gopal liked the place and in a few minutes he became friends of all the children.

In a few days Gopal mixed with those people so deeply that he forgot who he was or from where he came. He began to act exactly the same as the others.

It was a tribe of gypsies. The sannyasin was the chief of the gypsies. This tribe kept everything secret. Only those who were initiated into the tribe knew the secrets of how they got food, where they went and what they did. Even the children would not tell about their work. All the members—male, female and children—were supposed to give their earnings to the chief. They had no right to keep anything for themselves. But the chief would give them a share of the income. Those gypsies would call themselves disciples of a great saint Gorakhnath, who lived several hundred years ago and who had all powers (siddhis). Saint Gorakhnath started a sect called the Nath sect, and several saints of the Nath sects attained supernatural powers. No one knows how this gypsy tribe claimed to be the disciples of the Nath sect. But all the men in the sect would dress like monks of the Nath sect.

In the sect there was a rule that all females belonged to the chief. The chief would allow a woman to live with a man if his work pleased the chief, and the woman would be given to him as a reward for a certain period of time. All children were supposed to be the children of the chief.

Gopal was given a job of watching the horses, taking them to jungles for grazing, washing them in the river, and cleaning the barn. He was not alone in this duty. There were five more children of his age. Some were a couple of years older, but Gopal was the strongest and biggest of them all. His complexion was fair. He was tall and slim, with a thin, long nose and big black eyes, whereas the others were small and bulky, with dark skin, a wide, fat nose and small eyes. One girl was an exception. She was also different in body build, color and nature. Her name was Paro. She was very beautiful, shy, and would not mix with others in playing. She was one year older than Gopal, so she considered him as her younger brother.

In one year Gopal became a perfect horseman. He could compete with even the grown-up men, who were considered experts in horsemanship. For Gopal it was natural to control a horse. He inherited horsemanship from his Rajput (kingly) family. When a seed finds an appropriate soil it grows by itself. Gopal's warrior nature began to sprout. Those gypsies would train their children in the arts of self-defense like sword fighting, lance fighting, staff fighting and wrestling. Everyone was supposed to do physical exercises early in the morning with certain breathing exercises. Some techniques were secret and only the selected gypsies would do them inside a room where no one under sixteen years of age was allowed to go.

The chief noticed that Gopal was coming out like a diamond from the dirt. No one was equal to him in anything. He was very attracted to Gopal but wondered whether he would stay in the tribe or run away. So the chief started giving him special attention. He was given good food, a better place to live, and was put in charge of the horses.

In his mind Gopal had completely accepted the tribe. Sometimes he would feel bad because he was not allowed to attend certain meetings, whereas some boys of his age were allowed. He guessed that there was some secret because he attended a few ceremonies in which the boys who were initiated were told that now they were entitled to know all the secrets of the tribe.

Two years passed and Gopal's desire to get initiated into the tribe began to grow more and more. All his friends were already initiated into the tribe. Even though he was not initiated, still he was considered and accepted by all the young kids as their leader.

One day the chief arranged a contest of all the men and boys. In the contest Gopal was the only person who could ride standing on the back of the horse, holding a glass of milk without spilling it. He could hit a pinpoint target with a lance while riding a horse. In swordfighting he could swing two swords so fast that people would see a star of light and not his body.

The chief saw all his skills and thought that Gopal was the only one who could take his place and lead the tribe quite safely. So he called Gopal one day and said, "Gopal, do you want to go back to Banares?" Gopal said, "No. I don't want to go there anymore. I am very happy here. I want to get initiated into the tribe. All my friends are already initiated. I don't understand why I am not initiated yet."

The chief said,"Gopal. you are the most intelligent, handsome, strong and skillful boy in the tribe. There is no doubt of it. But I did not initiate you because I did not know if you want to live in the tribe for your whole life. Once a person is initiated in this tribe, then he can't leave the tribe. If one leaves the tribe then do you know what punishment he gets? *Death."*

Gopal said, "I honestly tell you that I want to be in this tribe and I'll never leak out the secrets as long as I am alive in this world."

The chief said, "In that room there is a figure of our Guru (preceptor), Saint Gorakhnath. When one gets initiation he takes a vow in front of that figure that he will keep the vow."

Gopal had much love and respect for the chief. He said, "Sir, for me to take a vow in front of you is enough, but if you want me to take a vow in front of the figure of Saint Gorakhnath, then I'll obey your orders."

The chief said, "Gopal, I love you very much and I want you to get initiated, but I give you one more chance to think and make a final decision before you take the vows. I don't want to see you as a deserter or killed by the tribe. I am very attached to you. I want you to live in the world happily and with much respect anywhere you live. In this tribe you have to do several dangerous things and sometimes bad things, too. So you should not decide it in haste. Let me know tomorrow if you really want to be initiated in the tribe, even though there are several bad things in the tribe."

Gopal left for his room. He could not sleep all night. He thought, "What bad things can they do? They earn their livelihood somehow. All the people are very kind and loving. The chief himself loves me so much. Then how could I leave the tribe? I can't live in the world by begging food. I need friends. I need society and I need support. Here I have everything."

Next morning Gopal went straight to the chief. On the way he met Paro. She heard about Gopal's getting initiation. When she saw him running she said, "Gopal, where are you going?

I heard you are getting initiation." Gopal was in a hurry and without looking at her face he said, "Yes, I have finally decided to get initiation," and stepped fast. Paro wanted to yell and call him to talk about it, but she was afraid that the chief would be suspicious of her, so she returned to her place with a heavy heart and a sad face.

Gopal entered the chief's room and said, "Sir, I have made my final decision. I'll get initiation," and he bowed to the chief and ran back to his room.

THE CHIEF fixed an auspicious day for Gopal's initiation. Because he had selected Gopal as his heir, he wanted to celebrate his initiation in a special way. He ordered the tribe to decorate all huts and clean up the ground. All the people of the tribe collected there. Those who were gone to the cities for business purposes also returned to be in the ceremony.

They made a huge geometrical pattern (mandala) outside on the ground and decorated it with different colors, and then they collected firewood and placed it in the middle of the mandala. From the early morning the drums started beating and the women started singing tribal songs. Gopal dressed in new clothes, and all others decorated themselves with paints, flowers, beads and feathers. The horses were also decorated and a team of nine horsemen performed their dance with the beat of drums.

The firewood was lighted and everyone started dancing and playing their instruments. The chief stood up and blew his conch shell and rang a bell. The drum and dance stopped. The chief said, "Listen, my tribesmen, women and children. This is a very auspicious day because I am initiating Gopal into our tribe. I tell you that when I brought this boy here I decided to make him my heir if he would take initiation into the tribe.

I hope our preceptor Gorakhnath granted my desire. That's the reason we are celebrating the initiation ceremony of Gopal with much enthusiasm. Now we take three rounds of this sacred fire which will purify our body and mind." The chief, Gopal and the whole tribe took three rounds of the sacred fire clockwise and then the chief said, "Now we all should go into the temple of Saint Gorakhnath for the final vows." The chief and the tribe went to the temple, where everyone took their seats peacefully.

The chief took Gopal to a dais where the figure of Saint Gorakhnath was standing. The chief said, "Gopal, repeat this vow three times facing the figure: 'I take a vow in front of Guru Gorakhnath. The sacred fire is the witness. I'll not leak out any secret of the tribe after I am initiated into the tribe. May Guru Gorakhnath give me strength to keep my vows until death'."

Gopal repeated the vow three times and then bowed to the figure of Guru Gorakhnath by lying flat on the ground three times. Then the chief gave him a seat by his side and said, "Now you will be initiated into the tribe."

He poured something in an earthen jar and took one sip of it and gave it to Gopal to take a sip. After taking a sip, Gopal gave it back to the chief who took one more sip and then gave it to the others to take a sip from it.

The chief, with a loud voice, proclaimed, "Now Gopal's name is Vajranath. He is my heir. In case I die or something bad happens to me, then the whole tribe will obey Vajranath." All the women, turn by turn, put garlands on Vajranath's neck and decorated him with paints.

Now they all were getting intoxicated from drinking that liquid, so the chief ordered them to beat the drums and start singing and dancing. All night the tribe sang and danced, and in the morning all lay there on the floor senseless. Paro only pretended to take a sip so she was not intoxicated. She noticed Gopal was completely senseless. She felt very bad about it and wanted to take him to his room, but she was afraid of the chief. She went close to him and wiped his face with a wet cloth and fanned him. Vajranath shook his head and before he became conscious Paro left the room.

Vajranath came to his senses but his head was hurting. He left for his room. On the way he saw Paro standing with tears in her eyes. She said, "Gopal, take a bath with cold water. You will feel better."

Vajranath did not like her to call him Gopal. He said, "Paro, do you know I was initiated into the tribe last night and my name is Vajranath." Paro said, "Yes, I know." She could not stop her tears, so she left for her hut very quickly.

Vajranath saw her rushing to her hut and could not understand why she was sad and crying. "She should be happy that I am initiated into the tribe. Probably she is jealous of me. But she always favored me over others. I don't understand why she is in pain. Maybe the chief was angry at her for some reason."

Vajranath took a cold bath in the river. He swam for a long time and felt refreshed. He came to his hut and rested for some time. At night the chief called him and said, "Vajranath, I'll teach you several magic tricks, several herbs to cure sicknesses and snake bites, sacred words (mantras) to drive out ghosts and cure people who are possessed by ghosts. I'll teach you how to catch snakes and train them. Every night you should come to me to learn all these things."

Vajranath began to learn all those things from the chief. For him the chief was a sannyasin and he would obey his orders faithfully. After teaching all this knowledge the chief said, "Vajranath, now you are allowed to make money for the tribe. I give you Paro as your co-worker. You first will go with another couple to learn how to work in the cities, and then you and Paro can do it by yourselves."

Vajranath bowed to the chief and left for his room. Next morning he saw Paro and one couple waiting for him outside. The other man, whose name was Ranganath, was two years older than Vajranath and had much experience in making money. So he said, "Vajranath, let's go. Paro is in your team. We four will work together. Don't forget to take your flute and drum."

Vajranath came out with his bag and an umbrella, and was dressed in orange robes. He said, "Let's go. I don't know anything about the work, but I'll do whatever you say."

[105

Ranganath said, "Don't worry. Paro knows everything. She was on my team twice before. Even if we are separated in the cities, Paro can tell you what to do. Do you know we are going to Allahabad? There is a big winter festival. Millions of people come there. We can make much money in different ways. I'll show you how we make money."

The group left for a railway station, from where they took a train to Allahabad. They camped at the bank of the Ganga, away from the crowd. Ranganath dressed as a psychic person and told the others to address him as if they were part of the crowd, and he would tell their past and future. In this way others would come. He sat down close to a bridge and spread his books, a map of the hand, a pair of dice and some kind of mandala to attract people. Slowly people surrounded him and a woman with tears in her eyes went closer and said, "Sir, why am I so miserable?"

The psychic looked at her with a sharp eye and said, "Close your eyes." The woman closed her eyes.

The psychic said, "Do you see a goat?"

The woman said, "Yes, Sir."

"Do you see the goat is grazing leaves of a tree?"

The woman said, "Yes, Sir."

The psychic said, "Do you see a woman hit the goat with a rock and the goat died?"

The woman said, "Yes, Sir."

The psychic said, "Do you know it's you? Your pain is only due to the killing of that goat. I can help you. This is an amulet you have to wear and your pain and fear will go away. You can donate anything you want." The woman took the amulet and donated her golden necklace.

Then another woman came and the psychic said, "Your name is Paro, isn't it?" The woman, with folded hands, said, "Sir, you are right, but I want to know my future. Will you please read my hand?"

The psychic read her hand and said, "You will be very rich in a few days. But beware of bad people." He told her that for protection from bad people she should wear an amulet, and he gave her a different kind of amulet. The woman donated money to him.

After that, one person after another came to the psychic and donated money. Vajranath noticed that his friend Ranganath had made much money very easily.

Vajranath went to another place, and dressed as a medicine man. He put some herbs on a sheet and started playing his drums. People collected but he found that he could not make much money by selling herbs. So he went back to where he was staying and rubbed ashes on his whole body. He put on only one loincloth and went back to the festival.

Vajranath buried himself in the sand up to his neck and closed his eyes. The crowd collected around him. Paro was also there and she pretended as if she couldn't see clearly. She went closer and bowed to the head and said, "Oh, Reverend Sir. I am a young woman. Please take mercy on me. I am losing my eyesight. I am a poor lady. If I lose my eyes, then how can I earn my living? I know you are all-powerful and your words can cure my eyes. Please, Sir, take mercy on me."

The head gently opened its eyes and with a deep voice said, "Oh pious lady, I am meditating here. Since you are in distress, I tell you that by the grace of God your eyes will be all cured within seven days." The head again closed its eyes. The woman rubbed her eyes and said, "I am already cured! I am already cured!" The head opened its eyes and said, "Your faith in my words can cure it faster. Now you can go."

The woman donated all her money happily and left. Seeing this, a few other sick people prayed to be cured, and then more and more people requested to be cured. By evening there was a huge pile of money and jewelry.

Meanwhile Ranganath collected all his money and left for his place. Then he, too, wore ashes and put on a loincloth and went to the festival. The two women remained at the camp with all the money.

Ranganath saw Vajranath's head and the heap of money. He went closer and said, "Brother, it's enough. You can't cure everyone today. You have to take care of your body, too." He collected the money in a sheet and removed the sand. Vajranath came out from the ditch and hugged his brother. They took the money and went to their camp.

In this way, each day they disguised themselves and made

money. In seven days they collected so much money that it was enough for the tribe's expenses for three months. So all four decided to go back to their home.

They left the city area and camped outside in a secluded place where each team divided their earnings. Ranganath was greedy. He said, "The festival goes on for a month. We can make much money. Vajranath, if you want to go home then go with Paro. I guess we two will stay for a couple of days more." Vajranath said, "It's okay. We can stay here and wait for you."

Ranganath and the woman left for the city again and Vajranath and Paro made a tent out of the umbrella and a sheet of cloth and stayed there.

Inside Paro there was a great hostility against the tribe. Outwardly, she was very calm and loving. She never liked the tribal activities but she had no way to run away or stand up against the chief. She knew if the chief saw a little sign of hostility in her she would get killed. She loved Vajranath very much and did not want him to get initiated into the tribe. But she could not stop him.

At night Paro held Vajranath's hand and said, "Gopal, I love you. I did not want you to get initiated into the tribe. These people are thieves! They do all kinds of bad things—pickpocketing, prostitution, gambling, cheating and even killing. When the chief brought you to the village, I thought some day we both would run away from their trap and now I see my hope is all shattered. Gopal, I was not born in this tribe. I was brought in just as you were. I remember that I was a little girl and following my mother in a street. Some man came and gave me a flower. I smelled the flower and I could not walk fast and could not even talk. I saw my mother going ahead and then I found myself here. I don't remember the place, but I remember it was in Banares. My house was in a lane, a big three-story house. I had two older brothers. I don't remember about my father at all. I have a faint idea of my mother."

Vajranath said, "Paro, why do you call me Gopal? Gopal is dead. I am Vajranath, a part of the tribe. I have taken vows to be honest with the tribe. I know about your feelings for me, but what can I do? I never thought that I'd make money by cheating. I don't like these things either. Do you think I'll run away with you and deceive the tribe?"

Paro said, "I expected that, and now you can't. If you do, then you will get killed. I don't want you to get killed. You are my life. Neither can I run away by myself, nor am I ready to leave you. So my fate is tied up with you. I'll go with you anywhere you go. I know the chief loves you as his own son. He will do whatever you say. I want you to choose me for your team and never leave me."

Vajranath said, "Paro, I also love you and I want you to be with me. I give you my word that I'll never leave you and if there will be a choice, I'll choose you over all others. But I'll never break my vows, even at the risk of my life."

Vajranath and Paro waited there for two days, but Ranganath and the woman did not come. Greedy Ranganath started a gambling booth in the city at night with prostitution to make lots of money. But at night a fight started among the gamblers and one man got killed. The police raided the place and Ranganath and the woman got arrested.

WHILE VAJRANATH and Paro collected all their things and packed them they saw Ranganath and a woman sitting in a police van, heading toward their village. Paro said, "Look! They both are arrested. The van is full of armed police. I think Ranganath has told them the whereabouts of the tribe. It means everyone there will be arrested and jailed. What do you think now?"

Vajranath was shocked to see them arrested. He could not determine what to do. He said, "Let's go now. If he has given the secret of the tribe, then it's his problem. I'll go back to the tribe no matter what happens."

Paro said, "Gopal, don't jump into the fire. We have money and we are free. We can go anywhere. I am with you and we can make a happy life together. If we go there probably the police will wait for us, and if they take away all the people from there then we can't live there all alone. In both cases we have to leave the village. Then what's the use of going there?"

Vajranath very firmly said, "I can't break my vows. This money is not ours. We are not supposed to keep money by ourselves. If you don't want to go back then you are free to go anywhere you want. But first I'll go to the village and find out the truth."

Paro had no choice. She said, "All right. I'll go with you."

Vajranath started walking off the road and Paro followed him. They reached a small railway station from where they took tickets for Banares, but they got off somewhere at a small station. From that station they took a footpath and walked for several hours in the middle of a jungle. When they reached close to the village Paro said, "Wait. First listen to see if there is anyone there—children, horses, cows. If anyone is there, we can hear their sounds." They carefully tried to listen but they could not hear anything. Vajranath climbed a tree and saw that the huts were all burned down and he came down quickly and said, "Paro, there is nothing left."

In the meantime the night fell and both of them secretly went into the village. They saw a few dead horses outside. There was no man, woman or child there. Everywhere there was dead silence. Vajranath said, "It seems the police and the tribe fought with guns and they killed the horses so that no one would escape. God knows how many got killed and how many were arrested."

Paro said, "The police will chase us. They will know that two people from the tribe are still at large."

Vajranath filled with anger. His young age and his warrior's blood in his veins began to boil. He said, "Had I been here I would have fought to death and not let the chief be arrested." He entered the chief's place which was all burned down and sat there.

Paro said, "Gopal, why are you waiting here now? Nothing

is left here and we have to leave for some other place. It's foolish to stay in a house which is burning. We have enough money and we can start a new life somewhere."

Vajranath said, "Paro, I can't break my vows." He opened the secret door which was underground and threw all the money and jewelry inside and closed the door. He said, "This money belongs to the tribe and Vajranath has no right to keep the tribe's money. Vajranath has fulfilled his duty. The secret of the tribe will remain with Vajranath and Vajranath is dead. I am Gopal now. Paro, let's go now."

Paro did not like to lose the money which was earned by them and there was neither chief nor tribe to receive it. She thought it was foolish to throw the money into dirt like that, whereas Vajranath thought that by taking money he would break the vow. Also Vajranath couldn't die if he used that money which was earned by the teachings of the tribe and for the tribe.

He said, "Paro, let's go now. We are free. Vajranath is dead and Gopal was not initiated into the tribe. He doesn't know any secrets of the tribe."

They both were in danger, so they decided to leave the place as quickly as they could. In the darkness the two souls started walking to an unknown destination. They walked all night and in the morning hid under a bush of berries. They were hungry so they ate as many berries as they could and slept there. Again at night they took their way. They were afraid of being caught, so they did not walk in the daytime. They reached a railway station but they had no money to buy tickets. Paro said, "Gopal, now what to do? We have no money. If we are caught in the train traveling without a ticket then the police will find out who we are. So we can't go by train."

They stayed in the railway station under a bridge where a few beggars and poor laborers were living. Next morning again the same problem of money arose. How would they get food? Gopal could earn money by showing magic tricks or by singing and making Paro dance, but he did not want to use anything related to the tribe. So he said, "Paro, let's go to find some work," and they left.

Paro was still upset about the money. She looked at him and said, "Gopal, that money was ours, but you threw it there and no one will ever use it. Now you don't want to make money by showing magic tricks, by selling herbs or by singing and dancing. I never accepted you as a part of the tribe, even though you were initiated into the tribe, because you did not know the activities of the tribe."

Gopal was trying to forget all the past but Paro was reminding him again and again. He very angrily said, "I am Gopal. I don't know anything about the tribe, money, magic tricks or herbs. Don't remind me! If you want me to go away from you, I'll do that, but if you want me to go back and bring the money then I'll never do that."

Paro was scared to see Gopal's anger and she said, "I don't want you to go away from me. I don't want you to go back and bring the money. I am very attached to you. I love you. Because of this trouble my mind is looking for a way to make money so that we can get food and get out of here by train as soon as possible."

Gopal at once cooled down and said, "I'm sorry, Paro. I also love you, but I'm perplexed. I don't know what to do. I got angry at you for no reason. Let's go on walking. It's better than staying in one place and doing nothing. At least we will reach somewhere."

On the way the passersby saw them and thought they were brother and sister. Both were tall and handsome, with the same kind of complexion. Someone gave them guavas, which were growing abundantly in that area. All the way they met people who offered fruits and food to them, and now they both got courage to get some job somewhere.

One day, while they were passing through a sugar cane farm, the farm manager saw them and asked if they wanted to work cutting sugar cane. It was a rough job but Gopal and Paro agreed to do it. They started cutting sugar cane, making bundles by tying the stalks together with leaves. The manager had a very good idea just how many bundles a laborer could make in a day. He did not have to watch them, so he would sit in his room or go to the market to gossip.

For a few days they worked hard and made enough money.

Paro wanted to work long enough so that they'd have enough money for train tickets to a distant place.

One morning, while Gopal and Paro were working in the sugar cane field, the manager came and said, "You both are very honest workers. You made sugar cane bundles equally as much as the others without knowing that I check the work of laborers by counting the bundles. Paro worked very hard and now I can give her an easy job. She can cook food for me and keep the house clean. The wages are the same. She will get some rest there."

Paro looked at Gopal and said, "Should I take the cooking job?"

Gopal said, "It's all right. In cooking you don't have to work so hard. Moreover, the house is not very far. It's in the corner of the field." Paro accepted the cooking job and left for the manager's house.

The day before they were ready to leave, Gopal was cutting sugar cane and Paro was in the house cooking food. He heard Paro screaming loudly. He thought Paro burned herself or the house had caught on fire. He left the axe in the field and ran very fast to the house. When he entered the room he saw the manager on top of Paro. Her clothes were all torn and she was struggling to get away from the manager. The manager could not overpower her, so he started choking her throat. Her eyes were popping out. Gopal could not resist his anger and with his fist he hit the back of the manager's head so hard that his skull opened up and he fell down on the ground. The blood started coming out from his mouth, nose and ears. In the meantime, other laborers reached there and they saw Gopal hitting the manager. The manager was dead and Paro, too. All the laborers began to yell, "Murderer! Murderer! Gopal murdered the manager and a woman!"

Gopal was still in a rage and his whole body was trembling. He could not talk. He only stared at the dead bodies with wide open eyes. The laborers were so afraid to go near him that they left the room.

The police came and Gopal was arrested. The laborers who saw Gopal hitting the manager became witnesses of the murder.

Gopal was now cooled down. He tried to tell the people that the manager tried to rape Paro and finally killed her. He tried to save her by hitting the manager but he also died. But no one listened to him and the police took him to prison.

Gopal was in the prison. He was in much pain because of Paro's death. He did not know what would happen to him, but he was not afraid of being sentenced to death. With Paro gone his world was finished. He did not want to live in the world.

After waiting for two to three months, one day Gopal was taken to the court and stood on the criminal's bench. The judge looked at the young man who had no sign of fear in his face, who was neither happy nor sad. He could not decide how such a man could kill two people. In the report of the police Gopal was charged with two murders.

The judge said, "Gopal, did you murder the manager and his house-mate?"

Gopal said, "No, I did not murder either of them. The woman Paro was with me, and the manager gave us jobs of cutting sugar cane. One day he asked Paro to cook food for him and said he would pay the same wages. We both agreed to it. But one day, I heard her screaming and when I went to the house I found the manager sitting on top of Paro and choking her throat. To save Paro's life I hit him with my fist on his head and he died. I did not want to kill him. I only wanted to save Paro. This is a true story and I don't care if the police charged me with two murders or if I am sentenced to death. I am already dead by the death of Paro." His tears began to fall.

The judge said, "I believe you, Gopal, but who was Paro? How did you meet her? I know you were from Rajasthan and came to Banares, but there is no past history of Paro. Can you tell me anything about her?"

Gopal said, "Paro was my everything. I can't tell how I met her and who she was. I can only say it was God's will that we met and we were separated."

The judge believed Gopal's story, but by not telling the history of Paro he got suspicious. He asked again and again, threatened him, pleased him and gave several kinds of allurements but nothing worked. Finally he sentenced Gopal to five years imprisonment.

Gopal was sent to Allahabad Central Jail. The shock of Paro's death shook his whole body. He became very serious, aloof and dispassionate. In the prison he did not care if he got food or not. Sometimes he would work and then get lost in his thoughts. But all the guards liked him because he was a harmless person.

Gopal was given the work of pulling water from a pool and filling the drums for use by the prisoners. It was a hard job but no mind was needed to do this work. He was strong enough to pull water with a bucket all day long.

Two years passed in this way and Gopal had accepted this kind of life, so he had no trouble living in the prison. One day while he was pulling water a tall man came, dressed in a prisoner's uniform with an iron chain fastened to both his feet. The prisoner drank water from the drum filled by Gopal. He then turned to Gopal and said, "Do you know me?"

Gopal said, "No, I don't know you. I never met you before. I have been in this prison for two years." The man said, "On what charge?" Gopal replied, "Murder. I have three years more to go."

The prisoner surprisingly said, "Murder! Vajranath, look at me. I am your chief. Don't you recognize me?" Gopal looked at the prisoner and said, "Oh, you are chief. How did you come here?"

The chief said, "I was transferred here three days ago." He then said in a stern voice, "Vajranath, tell me the truth. Did you tell the police about the tribe?"

Gopal said, "No. Vajranath kept the secret. The money earned by Vajranath and Paro is deposited in your secret room. Vajranath is dead. I am Gopal now."

The chief said, "Where is Paro? Did she tell the police about the tribe?" Gopal said, "Paro is also dead. She kept the secret as long as she remained alive. I saw Ranganath and the woman sitting in a police van. That's the only thing I know."

The chief said, "Oh, now I understand. It was Ranganath's team who leaked out the secret. God saved me from committing another crime. Vajranath, I decided to kill you with my own hands if ever I found you. God saved us both and I did not kill you with this dagger." He pulled out the dagger and threw it in the garden.

Gopal said, "You have already killed Vajranath and Paro. But Gopal was always innocent."

The chief said, "Listen Gopal. I love you as my own son. I chose you as my heir for the tribe. Now there is no tribe, but I still love you. I know you are an honest man who always kept his vows. Listen, I'll tell you a secret of my life: I don't belong to that tribe. I am a monk of the Nath sect and my name is Amarnath. I am a disciple of a most powerful saint named Baba Sundarnath. By my austerities and devotion and by the grace of my preceptor I attained several powers. I started to use those powers to fulfill my worldly desires. When I met this tribe they accepted me as their chief. I was trapped more and more in worldly desires and finally I reached a prison for the rest of my life. I am quite old now. It doesn't matter to me now if I am in the prison or out of the prison.

"You are a young man and after three years you will be out in the world and who knows, it may be earlier. I have experienced the world and I can say that all the worldly pleasures are pain. I want you to get out of this pain and attain peace. I was trapped in powers and could not attain peace. Being my heir, I want you to attain peace. When you are released from the prison go to Almora, a town in the Himalayas. From there go to Bageshwar. There you will meet a monk of the Nath sect who visits the temple on the new moon. He will tell you how to meet Baba Sundarnath. If you worship Baba Sundarnath you will definitely reach Him."

While they were talking the prison guard yelled, "Prisoner number 21, what are you doing there? Go to your cell!"

The chief said, "Gopal, probably it's our last meeting. I'll be removed to some other place tomorrow." Gopal secretly bowed to the sannyasin and started pulling water. The prisoner slowly moved to his cell, making noise by dragging his chain on the rocks on the ground.

Gopal worked for a while and then he began to think about Baba Sundarnath. He forgot all his past and began to dream about the future. How he would meet Baba Sundarnath was a question which was present in his mind all the time. He was so lost in his thoughts that he could not work in the prison any longer. The guards reported the matter to the jailer incharge and he sent Gopal to the hospital.

For several days Gopal remained in the hospital and then the doctor recommended that he be released because he had lost his memory and would stay all the time in a state of forgetfulness.

GOPAL WAS RELEASED from the prison two years early. When he came out to the open streets he was very afraid of people, cars, buses and crowds. Several times he was almost hit by a car because he was so lost in his thoughts about going to the Himalayas.

Gopal got his money back from the court which he and Paro had earned by cutting sugar cane. Now he had only one thought—to go to Almora. He asked a few people about a train that went to Almora, but no one could tell him because no train goes to Almora. So Gopal sat down in a train and decided to go somewhere. The train reached Delhi. In Delhi he found out from an army man, who happened to be from Bageshwar, that he could go to Kathgodam by train and from there by bus to Almora, and from Almora by foot to Bageshwar.

By being in the open world Gopal got better and was much more aware of himself. He reached Almora and from there he left for Bageshwar on foot. After walking for four or five days, Gopal reached Bageshwar and stayed in the temple.

The priest of the temple was a good man. He gave him a good place to stay when he found out that the young man was searching for a monk. He thought probably the young man would also get initiated as a monk.

On the new moon at midnight, while Gopal was sitting outside on the porch of the temple, a monk came and entered the temple. Gopal realized that he must be the monk, and stood outside at the door of the temple. When the monk came out, Gopal bowed to him and said, "Sir, I want to meet Baba Sundarnath."

The monk laughed and said, "I want to meet him, too. I tried several times to meet him, but when I went close to him he disappeared. I know he is living in an inaccessible Bhatkot mountaintop where there is a cave. He comes down to the temple sometimes and the priest gives him rice and ghee (purified butter), and he again disappears. I sat there several times but could not meet him. Tonight I am going again. If you want to go with me then don't wait any more. I'm in a hurry. It's a journey of three or four days."

Gopal had nothing in the temple. He was always ready, so he said, "Let's go." Both of them set out for Bhatkot Mountain in the darkness of the new moon. After walking for three or four days, they reached the temple, where they rested. They did not know for how long they would have to stay there. The priest was not there and the temple's doors were closed.

The temple was in a secluded place where people rarely visit. So the priest was also not very interested in going there. But he would go there on the full moon and the new moon, or any auspicious days, because on those days monks and villagers would collect there for worshiping the deity in the temple.

Gopal did not know anything about meditation or worship. Several times he saw the monk sitting with his eyes closed. He also heard him chanting something. His mind was always concentrated on finding Baba Sundarnath. In his mind he would visualize him. He would talk to him and he would worship him. This was his meditation, which was real though no one knew about it.

The monk said, "Young man, we came to this temple together. Now our paths are different. I'll sit in a room at the other end of the temple to meditate until the full moon. Baba Sundarnath is supposed to come to the temple on that day to get rice and ghee. You can go to villages to get food or you can do anything you want to do. If you want to see Baba Sundarnath, then come to the temple on the full moon. While

I sit in the room don't come there because I'll be doing some secret methods."

Gopal did not understand much about what he said, but he understood that he should not go there and he obeyed his orders.

The monk wanted to have psychic power by the grace of Baba Sundarnath. For that desire he tried to meet him, but all the time he missed. This time he was determined to meet him and wanted to stay in the temple premises all the time.

Gopal only wanted to see Baba Sundarnath. He had never thought of asking anything from him. He only wanted to know the path of peace. So he went to the temple and sat down outside the doors, which were closed. He had no thoughts except Baba Sundarnath. In the wilderness at night when jackals were howling close to the temple, owls were hooting and the bats were flapping their wings around his head, he remained sitting very calmly, completely concentrated on Baba Sundarnath. At midnight, all of a sudden the doors opened by themselves and a figure of light came out. The light dazzled Gopal's eyes and he fainted.

When Gopal came to his senses he found himself sitting in a cave in front of Baba Sundarnath, the same figure which he was always visualizing from the day the chief (Amarnath) told him.

Gopal burst into tears and grabbed the feet of the saint and said, "Sir, I am a sinner. I haven't done any good thing in my life. I am a thief, a cheat, a killer. I don't know how to worship God or how to meditate. But from the day I heard about you I could not forget about you for a single moment."

Baba Sundarnath, who had been keeping silence for several years, broke his silence and said, "Gopal, all that happened in your life was simply an illusion. I know you were in the gypsy tribe. I know the manager got killed and I know you were in jail. It was simply a way to bring you here by your destiny. Your parents named you Man Singh, a woman named you Gopal, the gypsies named you Vajranath. But you are none of these. You are my disciple from your past birth, and your name was Ramnath. Paro came into your life to show you attachment and her death taught you dispassion. Had she not come into your life you would not understand attachment and dispassion. Close your eyes and identify yourself as Ramnath."

Gopal obeyed his master's orders and went deep into a trance. He clearly saw that Ramnath was living with his master in a valley of Nepal. He saw the bamboo bushes around their hut. Banana and papaya trees were growing all around. For how long he remained in a trance no one knows.

When he came out of his trance, he bowed to his master and said, "Sir, now I remember I am Ramnath. I was in a dream and becoming so many men and you awakened me from that sleep of ignorance."

By the grace of Baba Sundarnath he attained his higher consciousness of the past life. All his supernatural powers began to bloom again like a lotus blooms when the sun comes up.

Baba Sundarnath said, "Ramnath, these powers are the cause of rebirth and pain. In your past life you already ruined yourself by these powers, and you went through many lives in one life. Now you understand how to stay away from these powers. The main aim is to be in peace and that is God. The powers are servants of a saint who dwells in peace, but one who seeks powers becomes a slave of powers."

On the full moon the priest came to the temple and all the villagers collected there. The monk also sat down in the temple to meet Baba Sundarnath. But people saw a young and very handsome saint coming down from the cave instead of Baba Sundarnath. The young saint came to the temple and stretched out the same bowl which Baba Sundarnath had used. The priest filled it with rice and ghee and yelled loudly, "Baba Sundarnath transformed his body into that of a young man. Look how beautiful he is!"

Ramnath peacefully turned his back and began to fly to the cave. Everyone saw Ramnath returning and said, "Baba Sundarnath is immortal. No one knows for how long he is on this earth to help people."

The monk also saw the young man and said to himself, "He came with me. Was I with Baba Sundarnath for all these days? Was he with me in a disguised form?" His emotions rose so high that he yelled loudly, "I found Him! I found Him! I found Him!" and went back to Bageshwar jumping, dancing and yelling.

People saw a monk in the streets yelling "I found Him! I found Him!" Some said, "He really found Him," and someone said, "Oh, he has gone crazy."

Spiritual Wealth

AMDEEN'S FATHER came to the valleys of Dehradun when he was only thirteen years old. Probably he had run away from his home in the mountains to experience the world outside. He was an illiterate boy, so his only means of livelihood was to work as a laborer on the farms in the valleys. He would work for eight hours on the land, and the farmer would give him food twice a day, but nothing else. A few years passed like that and one day while working on a farm he met a woman laborer. They became attached to each other and finally got married. The woman was smart, and realizing that her husband was working for these farmers without pay, she told him to ask for wages when he worked on their farms. He was a hard worker and the farmers did not want him to go away. They gave him a small piece of land which was never cultivated; it had been used for dumping garbage in the past.

    He and his wife built a hut on their land and began to live happily. They bought a goat for milk. The goat was a part of their family; all three lived in the same hut and slept on the bed of grass and leaves. By the grace of God the woman got pregnant and in due time gave birth to a beautiful boy. They named him Ramdeen, which means "given by Lord Rama".

Ramdeen's father had not gone to school. Now he realized that if he had gone to school he would be better off than a laborer. He thought that he would not make the same mistake with his son; he would send him to school—who knows but his son would earn lots of money—and he in his old age would be the father of a rich man. So he centered all his hopes around Ramdeen.

Ramdeen started growing. When he was six to seven years old his father tried to send him to school, but he had no money to buy books and clothes, or pay the tuition fee. He sold all his goats except one, which he kept for milk for Ramdeen, and he got enough money to provide clothes for all three of them. He was still working without wages for the potato farmers who gave him the piece of land. The land was his wage for his whole life.

Ramdeen's father began to worry that if his son didn't go to school he would also become a laborer on the farms and remain poor for his whole life. He decided to go into town and borrow money from someone to send his son to school. He thought that when his son got educated all his poverty would go away; so it was wise to bear all troubles now for his education. He went to Dehradun to find someone who could give him money for his son's education. He went to a rich man and asked him if he could lend money on the condition that his son would pay it back when he got a job after finishing his education. The rich man laughed at his foolishness and said, "You are a stupid man. Who knows if your son won't become as stupid as you are. You are born as a poor man and so is your son. In the world we need poors to serve the rich people. So go back to your village and drop the idea of giving an education to your son."

Ramdeen's father got very sad. He did not get money in the town, but he got cholera, which was spreading all over Dehradun. When he reached home he dropped dead. His wife also got cholera, and in a few hours she also died.

After the death of his parents, Ramdeen inherited all the property, including poverty. About the same time the goat gave birth to two kids, so again the hut was filled with four lives.

Although Ramdeen was only seven years old, poverty taught him to stand on his own feet. Several people died of cholera in the villages, so there was a need of workers everywhere. One of the potato farmers where Ramdeen's father worked for his whole life also lost his wife by cholera. He was in great need of workers so he immediately called Ramdeen to work on his farm on the same terms as his father had worked. Sometimes the potato farmer was kind to Ramdeen because he had lost his parents and the farmer realized Ramdeen's pain by comparing his own pain at the loss of his wife. But sometimes he would think that Ramdeen's father brought the disease, and he would blame him for the death of his wife.

Ramdeen's goats would go to graze in the woods by themselves in the morning and come back in the evening. He had no worries about the goats, and for himself he was getting food and clothes from the farmer. He began to feel happy and gradually forgot about his parents.

Four to five years passed and Ramdeen began to think more about the world. But in his mind the farmer was like his father, or sometimes he would think that the farmer bought him as a servant from his father so he would have to work on the farm for his whole life.

In the meantime the potato farmer married a beautiful woman and forgot the pain of his dead wife. But he had a beautiful ten-year-old daughter who would remind him of his former wife, and then he would get sad. His sadness was not hidden from the sharp eyes of his new wife. She began to get jealous of his daughter, whose name was Sulochana. Sulochana was not only beautiful, she was also very smart. She could market the potatoes better than her father. Her father was very proud of her and loved her dearly. His wife was beautiful, but not very smart. She had much anger and could not tolerate Sulochana talking to her father. The farmer knew this, and to keep them separate, he would send Sulochana to town to sell potatoes.

Sulochana and her stepmother would not see each other for the whole day, but at night Sulochana would come back to eat food. This was the only time when her stepmother had a chance to hurt her. She would put chilies and too much salt on the vegetables left for her. If she complained that the food was bad, her stepmother would scream and yell, "You blame my cooking! I work all day long in the house single-handed and now for my service I am getting this reward!" If Sulochana left the vegetables then her stepmother would yell, "You eat in the town. That's why you are not eating at home. You have no right to spend a single coin on yourself. For one who has cultivated a habit of eating sweets and delicious dishes in town, how can the food cooked at home taste delicious? You blame me for cooking bad food and don't blame your tongue, which always seeks for varieties of dishes. I can't please you."

The farmer did not want to tell his wife that she was wrong because he was afraid that she would start fighting more and would blame him for taking the side of his daughter. But it was hurting him very much to see that his daughter, who was doing all the business, was being hurt through no fault of her own. He wanted to keep them separate, but there was no way to remove either one of them. Sulochana was only thirteen years old and not yet a marriageable age. He was not prepared to send her to someone else's house to live; it was a very shameful thing for a father to do.

His wife, who at first was happy with Ramdeen, became jealous of him too when she heard that her husband liked him because Ramdeen's parents and his wife died of cholera at the same time. She told Ramdeen that he was a laborer who should work in the fields and never put foot in the house. It was difficult for Ramdeen to work there and not to step into the house, because he ate food there and had to do the dishes. Sometimes he would even clean the room of his master. But Ramdeen stopped going into the house. This increased the work of the farmer's wife, which made her more angry.

Time passed and Ramdeen was a sixteen-year-old man. He began to understand that the farmer's wife was jealous of everything, so he started staying away from her. He would leave at night after taking food. He would take care of his goats and repair his hut; sometimes he would dig up the ground to make the place look nice.

One day early in the morning Ramdeen went to the farm and sat down in the yard of the house. He saw Sulochana coming out of the house with tears in her eyes. Ramdeen stood up and was about to say something when the farmer's wife came out pulling her husband by the hand, yelling, "It's enough! It's enough! Now I can't live in this house anymore. I know you don't say anything, but in your heart you always favor your daughter. She blames my cooking, she doesn't talk to me, she doesn't even want to look at me. She only wants to go to the town to run around with men. God knows how many men are with her. I can't live with a woman who has such a bad character. She is no better than a prostitute!"

The farmer's tolerance crossed its limits. He yelled, "Shut up! You are blaming her without any proof." His wife immediately said, "What proof do you want? Don't you see that when she came out of the house this Ramdeen was waiting for her? As soon as he saw her he stood up. If he had not seen me coming out, God knows what they would do. Probably . . . I am from a respectable family—my father never allowed me to go out of the house alone. But your daughter goes to the town alone and all day long she talks with people. Still you think she is pure and a virgin."

The farmer looked at Sulochana and Ramdeen. Tears came from his eyes. He began to realize that Sulochana was on the verge of her youth. One day she would get married and leave this house. He thought, "If I try to convince my wife that it's her fault, she may leave the house and never come again. In that case I'll lose both of them."

Breaking the silence his wife told her husband that she could not live in the same house with his daughter; one of them would have to leave. "That should be decided right now. I am not going to listen to any more excuses. If your daughter has no fault at all, then you can live with her happily and I'll leave for my parents' house."

The farmer looked at Ramdeen and said, "Ramdeen, your father worked with me when he was a young boy. He was a hard worker and an honest man, and so are you. I want you to marry Sulochana. I'll give you some more land and you can live happily."

Hearing this his wife became very happy, but she said, "If your daughter gets married to Ramdeen it's all right, but I'm not going to allow you to give them an inch of land. What you have given before is enough." The farmer said, "Do you agree that Sulochana and Ramdeen should get married?" She said, "Yes, but once Sulochana leaves this house she leaves forever. Also, Ramdeen will not be allowed to work here anymore. I can't stand to see the face of that lad; he comes in the morning like a dog and hides behind the house to see your daughter. Get them married and let me live in peace!"

The farmer did not like her anger and jealousy, but he did not want to make her more angry and so he agreed. That same day Sulochana and Ramdeen got married. No relatives, friends or neighbors were invited.

The farmer knew that when his daughter and Ramdeen went to live in the hut there would be nothing to eat, so he hid a bag full of potatoes in a bush along the way and secretly told Ramdeen to take the bag with him. He put the clothes and jewelry of Sulochana's mother in a packet and told Sulochana to take it with her. It was evening and the sun was about to set. The family took food together and Sulochana and Ramdeen were ready to leave. Sulochana went to her room to bring the packet of her mother's things, but it was not there. She looked everywhere. It had disappeared. She did not say anything to her father, but left happily for her new home.

Sulochana's father loved both of the young people very dearly and today both were forced to leave him forever. He watched with tears in his eyes until they disappeared from his sight. His wife was happy; she did not care if her husband stood outside for the whole night looking after them. She went in the house and took a breath of contentment, as if she had won the battle.

Ramdeen pulled the sack of potatoes out from under the bush. There was enough for two people to eat for fifteen days.

When they reached home it was completely dark. There was no arrangement for light, not even anything to make a fire. Ramdeen inherited only one cooking pan, and it was hanging by the roof, covered with junk because it was never used by him after the death of his parents. The hut was full of goats. In fact the goats were the owners of the hut. They occupied the whole place and Ramdeen slept mostly outside during the summer. Now he was a married man and he needed his own place. That night they adjusted somehow, and the next morning Sulochana got up early and drove the goats out of the hut. She cleaned and made a fire in the center of the hut. Then she roasted some potatoes. When Ramdeen got up he saw the hut was all changed. He ate the potatoes and then said, "Sulochana, what will we do for the whole day? I can't work on your father's farm any longer and I have no work here to do." He became very restless and said, "For fifteen days we can live on potatoes, but after that what will we do?" Sulochana said, "These potatoes are not for eating. This is the only wealth I got from my father." She suggested that he sell some of the goats and buy food. But Ramdeen did not know what buying and selling was; he had never even seen a market. So Sulochana made him select some billy goats and they took them to town. It was the first time that Ramdeen had seen a market. He was very excited to see the crowds and people selling different kinds of things. Sulochana, who was skilled in trading, sat down at one place with the goats, and Ramdeen took a walk to see the market. When he came back all the goats were gone. Sulochana had sold them for a good price. They bought clothes, food and cooking utensils and returned home.

Now Ramdeen began to realize how much work there was to be done: a hut for the goats had to be made, the land was to be dug, the goat manure collected, and so on. Thinking about the work, he could not sleep well at night. He woke up early in the morning and started digging the land. He was a strong man and he had had plenty of experience in farming. It was the time for sowing potatoes, so both of them worked hard. The land had been fallow for several years and it was covered with goat manure. Sulochana and Ramdeen dug the earth deep and removed all the rocks. They worked hard for fifteen days to make the land ready to sow potatoes. Now the other work was to make a hut for the goats, who were growing fast. Sulochana knew people in the town who would loan her money when she needed it. In this way six months passed and the potato crop was ready. When the crop was harvested it was an extremely rich crop. By selling the potatoes Sulochana paid back all the loans and also saved a large sum of money. Then they cultivated more land which had been lying fallow. Every year their crop got bigger and bigger and their potato business increased. They became prosperous.

The farmers heard about Ramdeen's crop and they were surprised that in just three years he had doubled his land. Moreover, everyone in the town trusted him and was always ready to help him.

Sulochana's stepmother also heard about their prosperity and she got jealous. She suspected that her husband was secretly giving his potato crop to his daughter, because such a small piece of barren land couldn't grow so many potatoes. One day while her husband was resting she went to his room and said, "I heard that your daughter is earning much money by a potato crop. In three years they have made as much money as you make."

The farmer said, "Oh yes, they are very hard workers. You know my daughter is an expert in business. Her potatoes sold at much higher rates than others. The quality, shape and size of her potato crop is better than others. Naturally the customer buys her potatoes first, so she has no loss of rotting potatoes. Also her crop comes first in the market. I think the climate of that place is warmer, and there is water which they can use at any time to irrigate." His wife did not believe him at all, but she pretended as if she believed. She said, "I am happy that she is prosperous and they are living happily. After all she is my daughter also by relationship. I have to wish for her happiness." The farmer was very pleased that now his wife's mind was changed. He said, "Fate counts everywhere. We gave them nothing and, see, today they have everything. Next year they are going to build a new house for themselves. Maybe someday we will invite them to visit us." With anger in her heart his wife smiled and said, "Oh, yes, someday we may also go to visit their new house."

Now her suspicion that her husband was giving his potato crop to his daughter was strengthened. She said no more to him, but left for her room. The same night, when her husband was fast asleep, she went out. She was very angry and jealous. She decided to remove Sulochana from the earth, but she was afraid that she might be caught or Ramdeen would hit her. So she decided to ruin them by some other means. At midnight she set fire to their hut and the goats' barn and then she ran back to her place and quietly lay down in bed.

The hut and the barn were made of grass and bamboo. They burned up like gunpowder. All the goats were killed, but Ramdeen and Sulochana somehow got out of the burning hut. They had just one cloth on their bodies. Everything else was destroyed. Even the potato seed was burned.

SEEING ALL the destruction, Ramdeen sat on a rock and cried. Sulochana was also sad, but she had courage. She said, "What is left here for us now? Let's go somewhere else and start all over again. So many saints live in jungles; they eat fruits, roots and bulbs. They sleep in caves or under trees. They own nothing and they don't worry about anything. They are happy. Why can't we live like them?" "We can't do anything else!" agreed Ramdeen. "We have no place to live, no goats remaining alive, no food, no money, even the potato seed is burned. Everything is gone! Besides, your father will not allow us to work on his farm. For me it's not very difficult to live in the woods under a tree or in a cave because I was born in a poor family and have always lived with many hardships. But you lived in a prosperous way. You got everything you needed. I doubt if you will be able to lead the life of a hermit. I'm pretty sure that if you go back to your father he will allow you to stay with him, because he will understand the situation. But I can't go there anymore. Your stepmother hates me more than she hates you. She will never accept me as a human being!"

Sulochana said, "It's not the time to talk about the past.

Circumstances force a person to adopt any kind of living. Those hermits were not born into poor families—some were even princes who never stepped on the earth without shoes. So let's go before the sun rises. We have just one cloth on our bodies—how can we see people in this state?" Ramdeen said nothing but started walking toward the woods. Sulochana followed him.

Ramdeen's hut was about four miles from the village; it was hidden by a ridge of the mountain, so no one knew anything about them.

A few months passed and Sulochana's father said, "I haven't heard any news of Sulochana. I used to see her sometimes in town. I think they must be busy preparing their land for the potato crop. Maybe I'll go visit them." His wife said, "They are not poor. Now they have money they don't care to meet you anymore; and you secretly gave them enough potatoes to start their crop! Now probably they are busy in building their new house. I am no longer jealous or angry. It would be nice if we both went together to meet them." Her husband was filled with joy when he heard that his wife was no longer jealous. He said, "My dear, I always believed that some day your mind would change and you would accept Sulochana as your daughter. Finally the time has come. Tomorrow we will both go to visit them. I hope you will not hesitate to give her the packet of clothes and jewelry which belonged to her mother. I gave the packet to Sulochana on her wedding day, but somehow she forgot to take it. The other day I saw the packet in your wooden box." His wife said, "Oh, in my absence you search my things!" She smiled and then said, "Yes, I'm happy to give her things back. I don't need those things for myself. I don't even know how the packet got into my box."

The next morning they both left to see Sulochana and Ramdeen. When they reached their place they found nothing but the ash of the grass hut and some bones. The farmer said, "What happened to them! Their hut is burnt down—look at these bones! Probably they were burnt alive and no one in the village even knew it." When his wife saw the bones she believed that she had won the battle—both her enemies were gone from the earth. But she began to cry and big tears rolled down from her eyes. Her husband could not hide his pain and he burst out crying, "Sulochana, I could not give you anything. I was the cause of your pain. Your mother left you with me to take good care of you, but I could not give you love, happiness, even the jewelry of your own mother. I am your wretched father. Forgive me."

His wife began to burn with anger inside, but still she showed sympathy and said, "My dear husband, you did everything for your daughter. Due to your help they became prosperous. It was your potato crop which went to them. But you can't change anyone's fate. You loved your former wife and did everything for her, but you could not save her life. In the same way you did everything for Sulochana and Ramdeen but they were destined to die by fire. Now let's go home. Our grief will not give them life. It was all God's plan. We have to accept it."

The farmer could not understand if she was really sad, or if she was still jealous. He said, "Oh, they are gone and this is the end of my attachment to them. I could not do any of the things that I wanted to do for them for various reasons. Now I have only one pain: I could not return Sulochana's own things. I'll remain indebted to her for the rest of my life."

They both left for their farm with different emotions. The wife was happy that her husband would not be able to relate to Sulochana anymore, and her husband was sad that he would never again see his daughter in this lifetime.

The next day the farmer went to town and the news spread everywhere. People blamed it on different things. Some blamed the farmer for being a henpecked husband, and some blamed his wife for giving so much trouble to Sulochana. But no one could decide how the hut had caught fire. No one dared to actually blame it on the farmer's wife, because she always stayed home.

Sulochana and Ramdeen climbed the mountain looking for a place to live. They stayed under the trees, behind big boulders and in caves, but they did not feel comfortable anywhere. Sometimes Ramdeen would get depressed from not finding a suitable place or any work to do for the whole day, but Sulochana always comforted him, saying that some day their boat would find a place to anchor. She, herself, did not exactly know why they were wandering in jungles, whereas they could easily find a place to live in towns or villages. They both were young and strong, so finding a laborer's job was no problem. But their minds were not thinking at all about going back to their former lives. They had no aim of living in the jungles either, but Sulochana had heard stories about saints who lived in jungles and animals were their friends, birds would sit on their laps, and she was visualizing the same thing about themselves. Ramdeen had a totally different idea. He was thinking that they would live like tribal people who grow food, hunt and camp in different places in jungles. So they both were looking at places according to their own desires, and that was the reason they were rejecting places for one reason or another.

Finally they found a place. It was a wide cave. It was not very deep, but it was big enough for two elephants to stand comfortably inside. There was a waterfall on one side and a flat place on the other side. There were no trees to make shade, so it was a sunny place. Ramdeen liked the place very much and began to think how he would grow potatoes on the flat land, how he would bring water from the waterfall to irrigate and how he would carry potatoes to the market to sell. Sulochana thought the place was very peaceful and warm, with pure water. She thought it was a perfect place for saints to live in peace.

They collected dry grass and made a thick bed inside the cave. For food there were different kinds of wild fruits, like figs, plums, apricots, sweet potatoes and other kinds of roots also could be eaten. The jungle was full of herbs which were precious for medicines.

For a month they did not see another human being. Then one day they saw a man standing nearby while they were collecting herbs. The man said, "If you collect this herb for me I'll bring food and clothes for you. I'll come here twice a month to take the herbs you collect." Ramdeen at once said, "Yes, we can give you this herb if you bring food for us. It grows everywhere around here. We live in a cave close to this place."

The man was very happy; he was getting the herb almost free of cost. He said, "All right, tomorrow I'll bring food and other things for you and then you can collect the herb for me. But I tell you, don't give the herb to anyone else who comes here." Ramdeen said, "Oh no, don't worry about that, we will give the herb only to you."

Sulochana knew that the man was getting herbs very cheap; she could sell the herb in town and make lots of money. But she did not tell Ramdeen this, because she was afraid that Ramdeen would be trapped into making money if he found out how precious the herb was. Instead, Sulochana said, "Look how gracious God is. He is sending food for us right in this jungle. We don't have to go to the town to work or sell potatoes or goats anymore. We don't have to worry about sowing or harvesting a potato crop in time. We don't have to worry about goats not coming home at night. We are free all day long. We can collect a few herbs every day and in fifteen days there will be all a man can carry on his back."

A year passed in this way and they didn't see any human face except that of the man who was collecting herbs from them. They were away from society, away from the world and living in a peaceful state of mind. Ramdeen's mind was now changing. He had no desire to grow potatoes anymore, he had no desire to make money or go back to the village to start a new life. He was not even very interested in collecting herbs for the man. One day Sulochana said, "Do you know this herb is so costly that if we would sell it in the market it would bring more money than a potato crop? Do you want to start a business of selling this herb? You will see that in one year we will again be as prosperous as we were by selling potatoes." Ramdeen said, "Oh I don't want to go back to that life. I don't want even to see the face of any human being—even that man. I am happy here. I told you before that living in a jungle would be hard for you. I think now you are tired of this life. My dear, you can go back to your father's place if you want, but I can't leave this place now." Sulochana said, "All right, neither do I want to go to the village or to see any human being, so we should tell the man not to come here for herbs anymore." Ramdeen silently nodded his head.

Year after year passed and they both remained in the same cave, sitting in silence and enjoying the calmness of the jungle. They began to feel that they didn't need to use words to talk to each other because they knew each other's thoughts very well. All their communication was done through their mental waves, whether they were sitting together or far apart physically. One day Sulochana went out to dig some roots for food. Ramdeen remained sitting in his cave. A wandering monk reached there while searching for a place to live. When he entered the cave he saw a man with long hair and a beard already sitting there. The monk stood quietly and waited for the man to look at him, but the man did not look up. Instead, he began to move his lips as if he were talking to someone. The monk thought the man must be crazy since he was talking to someone who was not there. Nevertheless, the monk sat down in the cave to rest. Ramdeen was still talking. The monk got upset and said, "Why are you talking when no one is here? Are you crazy?" Ramdeen politely answered, "Oh, I am talking to my wife. She is digging roots on the other side of this ridge for our evening meal. I told her we have a guest and to dig out more roots to feed the guest."

The monk said, "I know all crazy people talk to the walls and say, 'This is my brother, sister, or wife'. I don't want to stay with a crazy man." He stood up and hurriedly left the cave. When he reached the other side of the ridge he saw a woman was actually digging out the roots. He went close to her and found that she was also talking to someone while no one was there. He began to think they were both crazy. That's probably why they were living in this jungle. The monk said, "Oh lady, to whom are you talking? No one is here." The woman lifted her head and said, "Oh, you were sitting with my husband in the cave. He told me to dig more roots because we have a guest. When you left the cave hurriedly he also came out after you, but he stepped on a thorn. Now he is trying to pull it out. I told him that I was coming and would pull out the thorn for him."

The monk ran towards the cave and saw that Ramdeen was actually trying to take a thorn out of his foot. He was very surprised to see all this. He bowed reverently to Ramdeen and said, "I'll pull out the thorn with my tweezers." While he was doing so, Sulochana arrived with the roots and sat down in one corner of the cave. They both remained quiet but the monk realized that even in their silence they were communicating, because soon Ramdeen left and came back with some more roots which had fallen from Sulochana's sari while she was hurrying home. Then the woman stood up, collected the roots and went out to wash them. She came back and her husband gave a few roots to the monk to eat. The monk respectfully accepted the roots and said to them, "I bow to your feet and accept you as my spiritual masters. Please forgive me for my disrespectful attitude. Will you very kindly tell me how you achieved this supernatural power? At first when I saw you talking in the cave I guessed you were crazy, but when I found that you were really talking to your wife I was very surprised. Also your wife told me exactly what happened in the cave." Ramdeen politely said, "We have been living in this cave for many years. Once long ago, my wife was sitting here all alone while I was sitting outside somewhere. She heard a sound inside her head. The sound became louder and louder. When I entered the cave I saw her sitting with her eyes closed, with no body consciousness. I rushed to her and tried to see if she was still alive, but when my head touched hers, at once the sound started in my head, too. The sound increased more and more and I sat down by her side with my eyes closed. After that, we don't know what happened. We can't tell for how long we remained in that state, but when we came to our senses, we felt a peace which can't be described. From that day we sit in this cave and listen to that sound which starts inside the head and then goes to the spine and then spreads all over the body. The sound starts coming out through the pores of the skin and vibrates inside this cave."

The monk jerked and cried, "Nada Yoga! This is the Yoga of inner sound current. You have attained everything. Your whole body is completely purified." Then he bowed to their feet, crying, "Bless me! Bless me!" As soon as his head touched their feet, he himself began to hear the sound and lost body consciousness. When the monk returned to his senses, Ramdeen very politely said, "Now this cave is yours. You need to practice more to tune yourself perfectly with the inner sound. We will go somewhere else. For us the whole world is a cave and a jungle." And he and Sulochana immediately left.

Time passed and the population increased. People began to cultivate any land they found with water. Some people in search of land reached the cave and found a monk sitting there. From that day the place became crowded with people who came to worship the monk. The cave was changed into a big temple and the monk began to live in a huge building. But no one knows what happened to Ramdeen and Sulochana. Are they living in an invisible body?

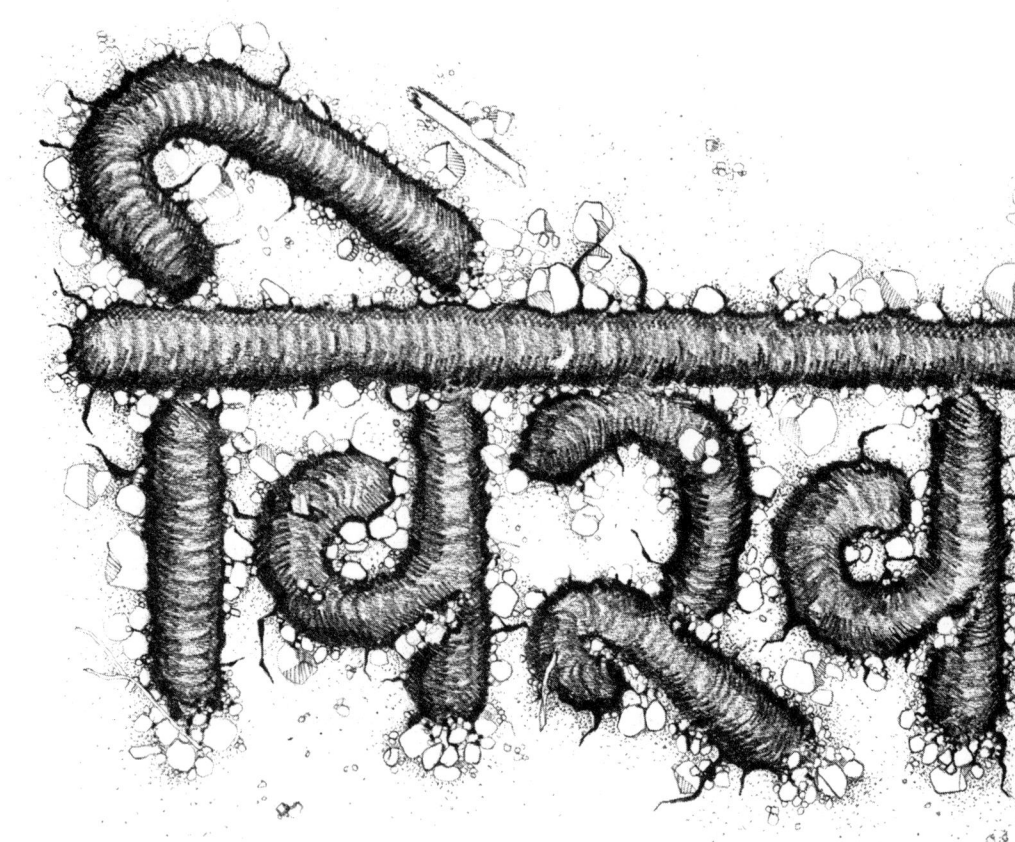

True Master

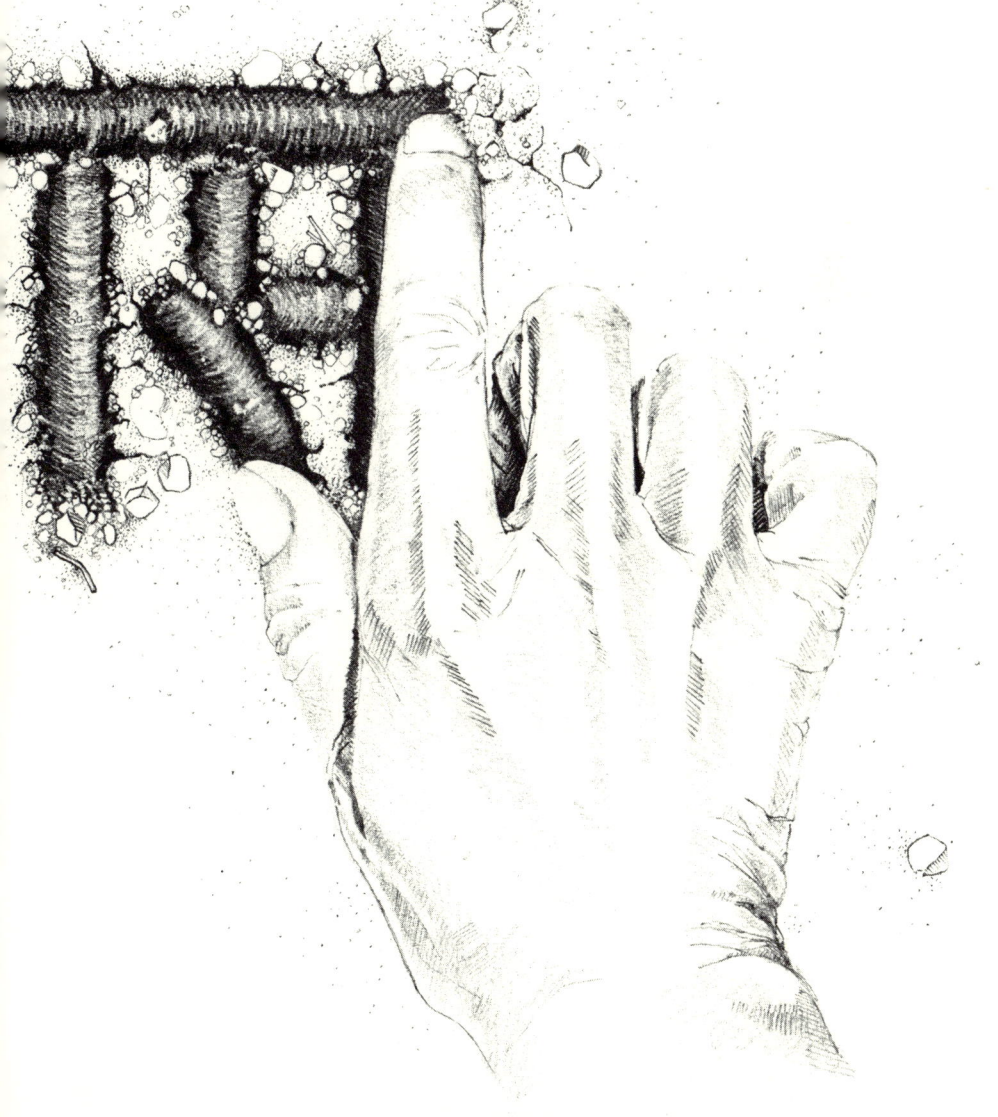

IN A VALLEY of the Himalayan Mountains, there was a family that had been living there for several years. The father, whose name was Sudarshan, had left his home town of Nainital when he was ten or twelve years old. He began to live with a few holy men who were traveling by foot to different sacred places in the Himalayas.

After visiting several places, the group of saints returned to their meeting place, the holy town of Haridwar. From there they all separated and went to their own places. Sudarshan had no special place to go because he was not yet initiated into any sect. He really had no idea of what a saint was, what a sect was, or what was the meaning of traveling to all the different places. He had left home only because he did not want to go to school and take responsibility.

For a few days, Sudarshan wandered in different places around Haridwar; then fortunately he met an old man who was kind and very learned in Sanskrit. The man saw that Sudarshan had a good mind and that he could be a good scholar. He told Sudarshan to live with him and that he would give him food and would teach him Sanskrit. Sudarshan was very tired of traveling and he was eager to find some place where he could live happily. So he agreed to the old man's suggestions.

Sudarshan lived for eight years with the old man. He learned Sanskrit and read all the scriptures. Gradually the learned people around Haridwar began to appreciate Sudarshan's ability in explaining the meaning of the scriptures. Sudarshan was happy and he almost forgot about his parents and birthplace.

One day the old man said, "Sudarshan, listen. Now you have two possible paths: either take the vows of sannyasa (renunciation) or get married to a girl and do your household duties while you continue searching for God."

Sudarshan was very intelligent. He knew perfectly well how difficult it was to take the vows of sannyasa and fight against desires. He did not want to cheat himself, so he replied:

"Sir, I learned all the scriptures from you, and I understand perfectly that to crush the desires by force is not an easy job. On the other hand, the householder's life is full of attachment and desires that create pleasure and pain; and also it confuses the mind when you try to understand yourself. But if I get married to a girl and practice seeing that the same God is in her and in myself, and if I separate the physical attachments from real love, then it will be easier to realize the truth."

Hearing this answer, the old man became very happy and said, "Sudarshan, you have understood the reality of life. Now I am going to give you my youngest daughter, who also is very intelligent and pious in nature. I'll arrange for the marriage, and then you can choose your own place to live."

Sudarshan got married to the daughter of his teacher. Her name was Sunanda. She was very beautiful and just seventeen years old. Still, she was fully acquainted with the duties of a wife.

After their wedding, Sudarshan and Sunanda left Haridwar and went north to live in the Pauri Mountains. A few years passed, and Sunanda gave birth to a boy. She named him Sri Charan. Sudarshan would write poems, stories, books on the scriptures, and in this way he would earn enough money to keep his family.

Sri Charan was growing up. When he was seven years old, his father was stricken by some disease and died suddenly. His mother received a heavy shock by her husband's death, but she knew that everyone will die. And no one can say when and where he will die. So she strengthened her mind and began to continue her duties as before.

Once, when the sun was about to set, Sri Charan became very sad. He began to weep. Sunanda thought that the boy was missing his father, so she took him on her lap and kissed him. Sri Charan hid his head on his mother's breast, and then slowly said, "Ma, where is this sun going?"

Sunanda said, "The sun always goes away in the evening and again appears in the morning."

Sri Charan again said, "Ma, why is this sky covering us like a box? My breath is choking. Can you take me out of this sky where I can get open space to breathe?"

Sunanda said, "My son, what are you saying! I can't take you out of this sky. You are hungry now. Take food and go to bed."

Next morning Sri Charan woke up and washed himself. He went to his mother who was grinding wheat to make flour. Sri Charan said, "Ma . . . you really can't take me out of this sky?"

Sunanda said, "No, my son, I can't. Forget it. Why do you ask such questions?"

Sri Charan said, "Ma, I am going." His mother did not pay much attention because she thought he might be going to play nearby.

After half an hour, she called Sri Charan but did not receive a reply. She looked here and there. All at once she remembered that his father had also left home at an early age. It could be possible that Sri Charan would also run away.

She ran down to a trail and saw Sri Charan going very fast on the other side of the valley. She yelled, "Sri Charan! Sri Charan! Where are you going?"

Sri Charan yelled, "Ma, don't worry about me. I am going out of this sky. I can't live here any more. My breath is choking."

Sunanda called, "My son, your father just died, and now you are also going away from me."

Sri Charan said, "Ma, I don't want to leave you. But if I live here I'll be choked to death. I tell you truthfully, I can't live in this box. I have to get out from this box!"

Sunanda was in a great dilemma. She could not think what to say, and Sri Charan was in a hurry. So with tears in her eyes she said, "My son, if you want to go, then I don't want to stop you. But I request that as long as I'm alive, you won't go very far from me."

Sri Charan at once said, "All right, Ma. I won't go very far." And he ran down the trail very fast and disappeared.

HE WALKED AND WALKED and did not know what to do, where to go. Finally, when the sun was about to set, he saw a watermill. He went inside the small watermill, where an old man was grinding wheat. It was getting dark and the old man saw that the small boy was all alone. He asked, "Where are you going?" Sri Charan had no reply. He was so tired that he had forgotten about the earth and the sky making a box that choked his breath. The man said, "Are you hungry?" "Yes," the boy replied. So the miller gave him two small breads and a cup of water, and said, "If you want to stay here tonight, go sleep in the corner. There is an old sack you can cover yourself with. I am going to my house." And he left before it got too dark.

Next morning, Sri Charan woke when the sun was quite high up in the sky. But he had slept like a dead and was completely relaxed. He came out of the watermill like a bird comes out of her nest in the morning. He washed his face and dusted off his clothes. He felt very good . . . like a bird out of a cage. He again continued his journey.

Now he was in a vast plain. He could see very far in the distance as he went on walking. Sometimes, on the way, he would meet some villagers who would give him bread and fruit. Again the sun was about to set and it was getting dark. Sri Charan thought that he should try to find a place to sleep before it got too dark, but there were no houses, huts or any kind of shelter nearby. He was a little afraid, but all at once he saw a big rock suspended over two other rocks so that they made a small cave. He went inside and sat down, resting his back on the rock and stretching his feet forward. He fell asleep at once. When he woke up in the morning, he saw two men standing outside. They asked, "Why are you sleeping there? Don't you know this is a place famous for poisonous snakes? Are you running away from your house? Or are you a thief?"

Sri Charan said, "I am going somewhere. I don't know where yet. I am not a thief."

Both of the men felt very kindly to the little boy and said, "If you want to live in our village, then come with us. We will give you food. You'll have nothing to do except to watch the cows of the village while they graze in the pasture. If you don't want this, then you can go ten miles south where there is a trail going into the jungle. Inside the jungle you will see some huts. A few boys of your age are living there and they practice Yoga exercises with a teacher."

Without thinking which plan was good or which plan was bad, Sri Charan replied, "I'll go to the huts where the boys are living."

One of the men said, "You are a tender little boy and the trail is very rough and full of snakes and wild animals. So go carefully and reach there before the sun sets." They gave him some roasted barley flour mixed with honey to eat. Sri Charan ate the food and picked up the trail to the south.

Now he was accustomed to walking, so he arrived at the huts early in the afternoon. He stood outside of a hut until a boy saw him. The boy at once told the others to come see the newcomer, who looked completely different from them. All of the boys surrounded him and asked him where he was going. Meanwhile the teacher came and asked his name and how he had reached there. The boy said, "My name is Sri Charan, and two men told me about this place so I decided to come here."

The teacher replied, "If you want to live here, then you have to obey all the rules. And you can't wear the clothes you are wearing now. I'll give you a few days to decide. Meanwhile you can rest here, and if you feel you can do it then tell me."

Early in the morning all the boys would wake up, wash themselves, and then do Yoga exercises. After resting for thirty minutes, they would recite prayers and then learn Sanskrit from the teacher. They all had their duties: cooking food, collecting food from villages, grazing cows, collecting grass and firewood, planting fruit trees, etc.

Sri Charan liked this life very much. He was feeling very free inside himself. He agreed to follow the rules, so the teacher gave him one red loin cloth to wear, one yellow cloth to cover his lower body down to the knees and one yellow cloth to cover his upper body. He said, "Sri Charan, now you are initiated into a Brahmacharya* order, beginners' stage. You have seen all the rules, and you can live here happily."

Sri Charan had some God-given abilities in Hatha Yoga. In doing asanas, he was the only one who could do them all, some even more perfectly than the teacher. After completing all his duties at the ashram (monastery), he would go to the river and perform some cleansing methods. No one had taught him these techniques, and he himself did not know what effect they might have. Afterwards, he would sit under a tree and meditate. Not one of the boys, nor even the teacher knew about Sri Charan's meditation.

One day while he was doing his cleaning methods, he drank several glasses of water and then vomited it out. Again he drank several glasses of water and rolled his stomach around in different ways; he did a few asanas and pushed the water out through his lower intestinal tract. Then he went in the water waist deep; he rolled his stomach around and pulled water in through his anus, and then flushed it out.

A saint was cooking his food on the other side of the river and was watching all of the activities of Sri Charan. As soon as Sri Charan had finished his meditation, the saint crossed the river and stood in front of him. The saint asked, "Who taught you all these methods?"

---

* Literally: "to walk with God"; a sect of renunciates.

Sri Charan was surprised and said, "What methods?"

The saint said, "All that cleaning by water, and that meditation." Sri Charan said, "Nobody told me or taught me any of those things. I started doing these things by myself. I don't even know what they are for. But I feel very clean and pure inside afterwards, and when I sit in meditation I totally forget my body and see only a light in my forehead." He raised his head and looked into the eyes of the saint. His whole body began to feel as if an electric current were passing through it.

The saint said, "My child, you are a very gifted person in Yoga. You did Yoga in your past birth and that learning pulled you to do the same in this birth. No one teaches anyone. We learn everything by ourselves. All the methods you are doing are perfect."

Sri Charan grabbed the saint's feet and began to weep with much love and devotion. He said, "Sir, I have a great desire to live with you and learn more from you."

The saint said, "My child, I have already accepted you. I'll tell you a few methods, but you have to live separately and do them by yourself. If you live with me, you will be dependent on me and your practice will not advance. But I give you my word that when I feel you need some change in your method, I'll meet you. A small tree can't flourish under a big tree. So do it by yourself and live freely wherever you want to live." The saint crossed the river and disappeared.

It had become very late and it was Sri Charan's turn to cook food. He was afraid that the boys and the teacher would be very angry with him. Sri Charan rushed to the ashram and saw that the boys had already cooked and served the food. No one told Sri Charan to sit and take food. No one asked why he was late. No one asked where he had been.

As it happened, when it got late the boys had complained to the teacher that Sri Charan was not obeying the rules. They were jealous of him. The teacher loved Sri Charan, but he was uncomfortable having someone there who could do asanas better than he could. So, after taking food, the teacher stood up; without washing his mouth or hands, he said, "Sri Charan, I don't want you here any more. You can go anywhere you like."

Sri Charan had nothing to say in his own support. He bowed to his teacher and all the friends, and left.

AFTER LEAVING the ashram, Sri Charan met several holy men . . . some were good and some were bad. But always he would live separately from them and would do his practices according to the saint who had accepted him as a disciple. One day, while he was roaming in the jungle, he saw a little hut on high ground, just two hundred feet away from a small river. He went inside the hut and saw an old saint wearing thick eyeglasses. Sri Charan tried to ask a few questions, but the saint seemed to be deaf and could not hear, or he would not listen. Instead, he showed different kinds of magic, like starting a fire without a match, simply by blowing through his mouth, or changing a rock into a flower. He told Sri Charan that if he would dig under a tree, which was three hundred yards north of his hut, he would find a large precious stone. Out of curiosity, Sri Charan went to the tree and dug in the ground. And there he really found a bright, shining stone. He took the stone to the hut and asked by gestures how the saint could know everything hidden under the ground. The saint said, "These are all powers given to me by God. I can see the future of the world."

Sri Charan was much impressed by this saint and decided to live nearby in a separate hut. One day the saint said, "Sri Charan, go and tell people about me—that I can liberate the human being from worldly pain, that I can forecast the coming of danger." Sri Charan went to the village to get food, and there he told about the miracles of the saint. Slowly the villagers began to visit the saint, and they were very impressed with his miracles.

Once, while all the villagers were collected there, the saint said, "In this Kali Yuga,* the greatest sin is sitting on one's gold. I'll make a sacred fire, and all should offer their gold to the fire in order to get rid of their sins." Hundreds of men and women started coming to the saint and they would offer gold ornaments to the fire. In this way, they would feel that their sins were burnt up and that God would give them peace.

Some days later, while Sri Charan was still meditating in his hut, he heard people talking and yelling. "He was a cheat! He was a cheat! He ran away with the gold! Where is the boy who is his agent? We will beat him!" Sri Charan came out of his hut and saw that there was no sacred fire. The ash had been carefully collected and taken away. He went inside the hut and saw that the saint was not there. He could not understand what was happening.

A few boys pushed him and hit him. Sri Charan was in his blooming age and so he could not tolerate this misbehavior. He pushed one boy so hard that he dashed against three or four others. Everyone was in a rage and wanted to beat Sri Charan. Sri Charan was also full of anger and stood in front of them like an angry cobra.

An old man said, "Listen, all of you! If this boy had been in partnership with that cheat, he would have gone with him. He would not sit here to get beaten up by people."

Then Sri Charan said, "I really don't know what is happening here. Where is the saint? Where is the sacred fire? Who did all of this?"

The old man said, "The man was not a saint. He was a cheat. He bluffed us all. He collected all of the gold we offered on the fire and ran away. You are innocent . . . we understand that now. But you should not live with such people."

For the first time in his life, Sri Charan saw how one can cheat others. But his faith in God remained unshaken. He

---

* The cycle of creation is divided into four long periods of time called yugas; Kali Yuga, the present time, is the last and least pure of the four periods.

said, "I tell you all, I'll stay at this place as long as I want. I don't expect anything from you, but I won't ignore any one of you either. God will give me food right here, I have faith in God."

The villagers begged him to forgive them for their misdeeds, and they left for their villages.

That same night, when Sri Charan was sitting in his hut, the saint who had accepted him as a disciple came and sat down. Sri Charan bowed to him with much love, but at the same time he had doubts as to whether he was being trapped again. The saint at once guessed his inner thoughts and said, "Tell me what is bothering you so much. Your mind is not in peace." Sri Charan related the whole story and told how he had become very angry at the villagers and had also pushed them very badly.

The saint said, "Sri Charan, you are a yogi. You should control anger. Now I will tell you the easiest method to control anger: 1) don't talk to anyone by mouth; 2) don't invite anyone to come to you; 3) don't tell anyone to go away; 4) reply only when someone asks a question. Otherwise sit in a peaceful mood. This is your next sadhana. I'll meet you when I feel you need my help." The old saint, who was the real master of Sri Charan, went out of the hut and disappeared in the dark.

VILLAGERS STARTED coming once again to Sri Charan. He had stopped talking. Whenever anyone would ask anything, he would write a short reply with his finger on the ground. He reduced his needs to a minimum: one blanket, one loincloth, and milk to drink if anyone brought it. He stopped eating grains, fruits, and all other things.

The villagers were much attracted to Sri Charan, so they would bring milk even if it were raining or snowing—they would feel it was their duty to feed Sri Charan. And Sri Charan was getting more and more detached from everything.

There was one old man whose only son had died when he was just nineteen years old. Suffering from the shock of his son's death, he would come to Sri Charan every day and bring milk. It gave him much pain to see Sri Charan sitting in the cold, eating nothing, talking to no one. He began to love him as his own son, and he would try to take great care of him.

Sri Charan now had a little beard, delicate moustache and long, matted hair hanging to his waist. Everyone respected him as a saint . . . he was no longer a boy in the eyes of the villagers. So that no one would disturb him, he would meditate at night and sleep in the day. His faith and devotion began to grow day by day, and he had no anger, hate or jealousy for anyone. The villagers built a huge hut for him where he could sit with people while they chanted spiritual songs.

One night his master came. Sri Charan bowed to him and said, "My master, I have no one else whom I can love. Whenever I meet you, my heart fills with joy. Why don't you allow me to live with you?"

The saint said, "Sri Charan, you have to realize the truth by yourself. I can cook for you, but I can't eat for you. Your faith in me is your master."

Having spoken, the master put his hand on Sri Charan's head. At once, Sri Charan felt an electric current running from the tip of his spine to the top of his head. He could not see a thing—only a brilliant light shone everywhere. He could not hear a thing—only the sound of Om...m...m...reverberated.

For several hours, he remained like this. When he came to his senses, he fell on the feet of his master with much love, thanking him for giving him such experiences. The saint said, "Sri Charan, it is already in you. I have done nothing. It is your faith that has done this."

Next morning, Sri Charan sat outside facing the rising sun. He was in peace. The bereaved old man came at his regular time with the milk. He saw Sri Charan sitting on the ground in the cold. He went near him and put his hand on his head. Sri Charan at once felt the same energy . . . same light . . . same sound. He became unconscious.

When he returned to consciousness, he saw the milk man sitting in front of him with tears in his eyes, saying, "What happened to you? I simply put my hand on your head and you fell to the ground!"

Sri Charan said, "Was it *your* hand?" Now he realized that his own faith was the cause of his bliss. He said to himself, "My master is always inside me." And he never desired to live with his master again.

Cave
of
Enlightenment

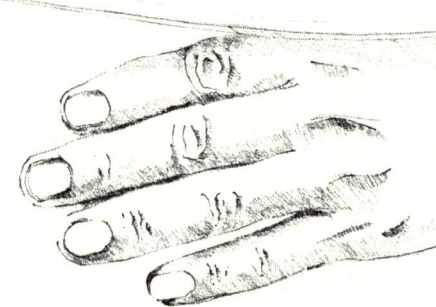

HARU Chand Mukharji was a rich man from the city of Calcutta. He built a large house in Ramchandra Mukharji Lane, where his forefathers had lived for several generations. That whole section of the city belonged to the Mukharji Brahmins, who were very proud of their high caste. They had always maintained their prestige by marrying only high caste Brahmins of their same rank.

Charu Chand Mukharji, who was well known as Charu Babu,* lived in his house with his three sons, one daughter and a cook. The cook was the same age as Charu Babu, and had been working for his family from the age of eight. He came from Bihar province, where his parents had left him, or they had died—he did not remember well—when he was very little. Somehow he reached Calcutta, and Charu Babu's father found him in a cremation place. Sri Mukharji brought the boy home, and from that day the boy accepted that place as his home and never left, even for a single day.

In his youth, Charu Babu worked as a manager in a jute mill. He earned good money, and after several years he was able to buy the same mill. His first son, whose name was Sunil, was

---

* Babu is a term of respect; literally: "Master".

twenty-four years old and had a degree in business management. Charu Babu engaged him in his jute mill as the treasurer. He wanted to train Sunil in all branches of the work so that he would be able to run the mill successfully after his death.

His second son, whose name was Vijaya, passed high school, but did not go to college. Charu Babu tried to bring him into the business, but Vijaya did not want to work in the jute mill. He was a poet. He would sit in his room, or go to the bank of the River Ganga or to some temple and write poems. Charu Babu did not know that Vijaya wrote poems because his mill work kept him so busy that he had no time to talk to him.

The third child was a daughter, whose name was Pramila. She was fifteen years old and was going to school. She was very beautiful, very smart and religious-minded.

The fourth child was a son, and his name was Sanjaya. He was eight years old and very free. He would go to school sometimes, but not regularly. He was the most beautiful boy in the family. Sanjaya's mother used to say that he would be just like his grandfather: tall, large-boned and strong, with fair complexion and a long nose.

When Sanjaya was only eighteen months old, his mother died after a long illness. Charu Babu was in his fifties at that time. The death of his wife brought much pain to him, but he was so entangled with his business that he had little time to think about her.

The management of the whole house was in the hands of the cook, even before Charu Babu's wife was dead. Purchasing food, cooking, cleaning, looking after the children—all was his responsibility. Charu Babu's wife had always been weak and sickly; when she came to this house after marrying Charu Babu, the cook was already in charge there, so she never tried to take things into her own hands. After her death there was no interruption of any kind in the management of the house. But the house was like a kingdom without a king, even though everything was going on smoothly.

Charu Babu felt that a house without a woman was like a deserted house. So he decided to get his older son, Sunil, married. One day he called Sunil and said, "Sunil, for seven or eight years since your mother died, this house has been without a woman. Pramila is now old enough to be married and soon she will also leave. Sanjaya is still a young boy and needs the family until he finishes college or gets a job and becomes independent. The cook is like a mother to you all and he is doing his best to keep the house together, but he is as old as I am, and who knows when the bird will fly away from the cage?* If you get married now, your wife can learn from the cook how to run the house smoothly."

Sunil thought a little and said, "Yes, I understand that a house without a woman is like a flower without fragrance. I am now capable of taking responsibility for a wife, so I guess I am ready to marry."

Charu Babu started looking for a bride in different parts of Calcutta among the families of Brahmins. It was not difficult for Charu Babu to arrange for a wife for his son, because he was a rich man and his son was educated, healthy, handsome and from a high caste Brahmin family. Several offers came from the parents of such girls.

Madhusudan Bhattacharya was an old friend of Charu Babu's from school days. He was among those who sent an offer for his daughter to marry Sunil. Charu Babu had not the time to search many places to choose a girl for his son, so he told Sunil to go to Madhusudan Bhattacharya's house to see if he would like to marry his daughter.

Sunil went to see the girl and found her well-educated and working as a school teacher. When the girl met Sunil she was not at all shy. They talked for some time on various subjects, and they liked each other. When Madhusudan Bhattacharya's wife asked Sunil if he liked their daughter, Swapna, Sunil very excitedly said, "Oh, yes. I give my word that I would like to marry Swapna." Swapna also gave her consent, and the marriage was arranged at that very moment.

Charu Babu heard the news and he was very happy that Sunil had decided the matter so intelligently and quickly. Now he did not have to bother about choosing among several girls, arranging marriage dates and running all over the place.

Sunil got married and Swapna came to her new home. Charu

---

* The soul will leave the body.

Babu's house again filled with a new energy, a new light and a new attachment.

Sunil was very happy and deeply in love with his wife. Swapna was an experienced teacher, and her nature was very commanding. Sunil was putty in her hands and he would do things according to her desires. Likewise the cook, who had been the manager of the house for almost all his life, was no longer free to do things according to his choice—Swapna would keep an account of the smallest coin, for the smallest expense.

Vijaya was very unconcerned about all household things. He did not join the marriage ceremony, and he never talked to Swapna. He would stay in his room and speak only to the cook about his meals. This was the extent of his relationship with the house.

Pramila felt jealous of her sister-in-law, because she loved Sunil very much and felt as if her brother were being kidnapped by some unknown woman. But she overcame this feeling because she knew that this is the way the world works. Some day she would also get married and take away someone's brother or son.

Sanjaya was as free as ever. He would eat, play and go to school according to his own will. For a few days he enjoyed Swapna's company, but after a while he was no longer excited by the new addition to the family, so he resumed his life pattern as before.

Sunil's wife, Swapna, did not like Sanjaya's freedom. She thought that if he were not disciplined, he could not finish school and, who knows, he might be trapped in bad society and ruin his life. So she started trying to control him. At first Sanjaya obeyed her, but when she started putting too much pressure on him, sometimes with hate and anger, then Sanjaya ignored her. It made her very angry and she stopped talking to him. It did not bother Sanjaya at all—he felt much better by not talking to her.

Swapna at first complained to Sunil about Sanjaya—how bad, disobedient and undisciplined he was. Sunil listened to his wife, but he thought it was simply a power struggle between Sanjaya and Swapna. He thought that some day they would reach a compromise by themselves, and so he did not say anything to his brother. It made Swapna still more angry and she said, "All you brothers are alike! No one listens to anyone. Why should I bother to discipline him? If he doesn't go to school, or joins bad company, it will not ruin my life!"

IT NOW WAS THE MONTH of October. Rains had stopped and the weather was not hot anymore. It was the best season for flying kites. Millions of kites were flying in the sky from morning until night. People were able to do different kinds of tricks with their flying kites, and sometimes they would bet on a kite fight. Sanjaya's favorite play was flying kites. He would buy a kite every day and fly it from the balcony of the third story. One day he pulled a torn kite down and went to his older brother's room to glue it. While he was fixing the kite, Swapna came to the room and saw Sanjaya sitting on the floor with paper and glue, fixing his kite. As his kite was all fixed, Sanjaya stood up and was about to leave for the balcony. Swapna said in a sharp voice, "Why did you come in my room? My room is not for fixing your kite. You have no right to come in my room. Get out! Get out!"

Sanjaya was very surprised to see the anger of his sister-in-law. No one had ever been so angry with him before. He had never heard before that he couldn't go in any room of the house. He said, "I always fly kites from the balcony, and I have always fixed my kites in this room. No one ever stopped me and no one ever told me that I can't come to this room.

There is no other place from where I can fly kites." And he stepped out on the balcony.

Swapna sprang at him with a scream and smashed his kite. She snatched the reel of thread from his hand and threw it down on the street. At first Sanjaya was wonderstruck. Then he began to cry. He had fixed the kite with so much labor and his sister-in-law had destroyed it in one second. There was no one in the house to console him, and Swapna was looking at him like an angry cobra.

"Why did you smash my kite?" cried Sanjaya, "I bought it with my own money. I did not take any of your things."

Swapna answered, "It's my room and this balcony goes with this room. I am your brother's wife. That doesn't mean I am a servant for all of you. I am not going to clean up your garbage."

Sanjaya said, "There is no other place from where I can fly the kite. Why can't I fly my kite from the balcony?"

Swapna got so angry that she shouted, "Don't threaten me with your crying! I have straightened out several boys like you in school." She grabbed him by the hand and pushed him down the stairs.

Sanjaya angrily said, "If you don't want me in this house, then I'll go somewhere else."

"Yes, go!" Swapna shouted. "Don't ever show me your ugly face again. I don't want even your shadow close to me!"

Swapna's words pierced the heart of the tender-aged boy. He came down crying to the street to look for his thread reel. It had dropped in a gutter. He picked it up, but the thread was all tangled and soaked with mud and water. He said to himself, "Oh, it's all useless." He walked away to the market, thinking to buy another kite and thread reel.

Sanjaya wandered up and down in the market to pass the time and also to divert his mind from the pain he felt from his sister-in-law's violent attack. At one place he saw a crowd of people collecting in a circle. He pierced into the crowd and sat down in the front row. There was a magician who was showing magic tricks. The magician asked if anyone in the audience could come up and help him in his show. Sanjaya was sitting right in front of him; he stood up and said, "I'll do it."

The magician said, "Come on, young boy. You are the most suitable person for this play. Will you be scared if I cut you into two pieces with my sword and again join you?"

"Will it hurt?" asked Sanjaya, and the audience laughed.

The magician hypnotized Sanjaya and asked him several questions about people in the audience. Sanjaya told several quite correct things about each person. He could tell even the name and from which place the person came. It surprised the audience very much.

Then the magician showed a few tricks with his cobra snake, which was trained to obey his orders. The show was finished and people donated money to the magician and left. Sanjaya also stood up to leave but the magician said, "Let me collect my things and then I'll talk to you." Sanjaya again sat down and waited.

When he was through packing the magician said, "Young boy, what is your name?"

The boy said, "Sanjaya Mukharji."

The magician said, "Oh, you are from a Brahmin family. Do you want to learn magic tricks?"

Sanjaya very eagerly said, "Oh, yes," and he began to think that when he would go home he would show magic to his friends and brothers and sister.

The magician then said, "Eat this candy first and drink a little water."

Sanjaya ate the candy and drank a little water and waited for the magician to teach him magic. He was expecting to learn everything in a few minutes. After a while he felt as if everything was circling about. He was unable to talk. The magician lifted his bags on his shoulders and started walking. Sanjaya had no sense at all and he began to follow him like a dog.

When he came to his senses he found himself in a hut somewhere in a secluded place, where there was a woman with two children. Sanjaya could not understand what had happened to him. How did he get here? Why had he not gone to his home? The magician gave him another candy and Sanjaya again became senseless. In this way he remained there.

At night the cook served food to everyone and waited for

Sanjaya to come, but Sanjaya did not come for the whole night. Early in the morning the cook, who could not sleep due to worrying about Sanjaya, went straight to Charu Babu and said, "I haven't seen Sanjaya around since yesterday noon. He did not come to eat food last night. He is not here."

Charu Babu said, "Oh, he is in his growing age. He must be with his friends. Why do you worry? He will come back. When he comes back tell him not to go places without telling you."

The cook said, "Sanjaya never stayed away before. He would go all day long but come to the house at sunset. I am very worried about him."

Charu Babu did not pay any attention to him, so the cook then went to Sunil, who was taking tea with Vijaya and Pramila. He said, "Sanjaya is missing since yesterday and you don't care if he comes home or not. Had his mother been alive she would be very worried. I am an old man. What can I do? I took care of all of you as my own children." He began to cry. "I can't break my attachment. Please look around. Bring him home."

All the children respected the cook as their father. In fact, if they got any fatherly love at all, it was from the cook. Charu Babu was always busy and never showed his love physically.

Sunil said, "Probably Swapna will know about Sanjaya. Did you ask her?"

The cook said, "No, I only told Charu Babu and he did not pay any attention."

Sunil ran up to his room on the third floor. Swapna, after taking her bath, was combing her hair. Sunil, in a perplexed voice, said, "Sanjaya is missing from yesterday. Where is he?"

Swapna, with a twisted smile, said, "Do you think I am a psychic or a baby sitter? I don't know where he is. In the morning when you left for the jute mill I saw him flying his kite from the balcony and I came up. I said, 'Why don't you read your books—go to school?' That undisciplined lad became so angry at me that he smashed his kite and threw away his thread reel and said, 'If you don't want me to live in this house then I'll go away.'

"At first when I came to this house I tried to discipline him but he never listened to me. He always tried to tease me by making my room dirty and by taking things from my room. So I stopped talking to him. Yesterday he was determined to fight, so when I criticized him a little he burst into a rage. I am fed up with this house. I was better off as a school teacher. I was independent. Here I am like a servant. I can serve you, but I can't serve your brothers and sister!" She began to cry.

Sunil did not want to argue with his wife. He felt that she was partly right, but he had much love for his brother, too. He also realized that Sanjaya had left because Swapna hated him. Sanjaya was brought up without a mother, so he had developed no love for a motherly figure. He said, "Swapna, it's not your fault. Why are you crying? He might be somewhere with his friends and will be back soon." He thought that if Sanjaya came back, then probably his wife and Sanjaya would solve their disagreement by themselves. So he left for his job.

Day after day passed, and then month after month. Sanjaya did not return. Now Charu Babu's eyes opened; it was probably too late to give a report to the police, but he filed a report anyway. For the first time Charu Babu's attachment came to the surface and he felt as if his heart were torn away. Sanjaya's image was present in his mind all the time. He became physically weak and was losing his memory, which created difficulties in the work of the jute mill. One day while he was working he got a sharp pain in his heart—it was the end of his work in the mill. He handed over all responsibility to Sunil and stayed home.

Sunil had worked in different branches in the jute mill and he was totally acquainted with all aspects of the work, so he managed efficiently. But now, due to his heavy duties, he had no time to talk to his wife. It was very hard for her. She was young and newly married, but she was away from her husband most of the time. Because of this situation her nature became more irritable. She began to think that it was all the fault of her father-in-law. Although she never dared to talk in front of Charu Babu, she was burning with anger all the time. She knew Charu Babu loved the cook very much, so she started troubling the cook. If he complained to Charu Babu, and if Charu Babu said anything, then she could tell her husband to separate from the family. But her plan did not work. One night Charu Babu got a very sharp pain in his heart, and in the morning he was found dead in his bed.

It was very hard for Sunil to manage the jute mill and his household single-handedly. Vijaya was already half crazy and would seldom come home; after his father died, Vijaya also disappeared. Pramila was in college and of a marriageable age. Now it was Sunil's responsibility to get her married. The cook was very old, and he told Sunil that he was unable to cook and work any longer. Sunil understood his old age and told him to stay in his room.

Six months after the death of Charu Babu, the cook also died. At the same time Swapna became pregnant. She was happy due to her pregnancy, but she worried about who would take care of the house when she gave birth to the baby. She said to Sunil that she needed someone in the house to help her with cooking and cleaning. Pramila had no time—she was in school and did only school work at home. Sunil could not find a maid servant, so he began to hide from his wife and stay in the jute mill even longer than before.

PRAMILA HAD A GIRL FRIEND named Bela Ray. She lived in the adjoining block, which was named Baranagar, where non-Brahmins of all mixed castes were living. Bela and Pramila never visited Bela's house as long as her father and the cook were alive. Now in the house there was only her sister-in-law, who was a very angry, jealous, selfish and hateful woman. Pramila never liked her before, and now that Swapna was pregnant, she was even more emotional. At times she would yell and scream without any reason. So Pramila started going to Bela's house to do her school work.

Bela had a brother named Pradip who was four years older

than she. He was a musician and a very handsome, shy and peaceful man. She had two younger sisters, also. Her father was a school teacher and her mother had died a couple of years before. All four girls would play in the house freely. Pradip would sit in his room and practice music. Sometimes he would go to the market and bring sweets for them, and then again sit in his room and sing or write songs.

Bela and her sisters took Pradip's songs for granted, but Pramila's heart would stir when she heard them. She felt as if her soul was captured by Pradip's melodious voice. Sometimes she could not stop herself and would go to Pradip's room, leaving her friends outside.

Bela was more interested in playing. She did not like her to go away from their games. One day Bela said, "Pramila, you don't like to play with us. You only want to listen to Pradip's singing. I guess you are in love with my brother."

Hearing this, Pramila's face flushed. She smilingly said, "Oh no! But I like to hear him singing. I've never heard anyone sing so well. You know, Bela, I also took music classes in high school. I understand how beautifully he sings. Moreover, what's the harm in loving such a handsome, kind and peaceful man? If it were my choice I would marry him, but . . ."

Bela said, "I know, Pramila, we are from a non-Brahmin caste. You can't marry my brother. If you married him the whole Brahmin community would make you an outcaste. Pramila, I also know that Pradip loves you. If some day you don't come, he asks several times about you. He doesn't sing. He sits outside to see if you are coming. He is a shy man, so he doesn't talk to you, but in his heart he has much love for you."

When Pramila heard that Pradip also loved her, she burst into tears. All her suppressed love came to the surface. She said, "Bela, do you know what my decision is? Either I'll marry Pradip, or I'll leave the world and become a sannyasin (renunciate)." Her tears were falling like two rivers. Her voice choked and she put her head on Bela's lap and began to sob. In the meantime Pradip came out of his room and saw Pramila crying. He said, "Pramila, what happened? A few minutes ago you were all playing. Did you get hurt?"

Pramila said, "Not in playing, but by the social rules." She knelt down and grabbed Pradip's feet and said, "Pradip, from the very first day I saw you, I fell in love with you. I hid my love so tightly that no one knew it. But it's a volcano. Some day it had to come out. We both know that society will not approve of our marrying and it is hurting me very badly. I also know that I can't live without you. You are the light of my life. Like a snake that carries a gem with him—if he loses his gem he strikes his head here and there and dies. I feel if I lose you I'll go crazy!"

Pradip held Pramila's hand and with much love he said, "Pramila, probably you don't know that I also was suppressing my love—partly due to my shyness, partly due to poverty and partly due to being a non-Brahmin. But I decided if I can't marry you then I'll never marry anyone else. I know you love me, but the social rules are so strict that if we marry by our own will, then society will make our life miserable. But if our love is real, then we can always be in the hearts of each other, even without marriage."

From then on Pradip and Pramila became very close, and sometimes Pradip, Bela and her two sisters would go to Pramila's house. A few times Swapna saw them sitting in Pramila's room, so she talked to them and found that they were non-Brahmins. She began to suspect that Pramila was in love with Pradip, although she did not know anything about them. She only wanted to create a fuss, so she started telling her neighbors that Pramila was seeing a non-Brahmin man. Slowly the news spread all over the Brahmin community, and people began to tell Sunil that he should get Pramila married to some Brahmin boy before she ran away with that non-Brahmin. Social pressure compelled Sunil to get his sister married to a Brahmin boy as soon as possible.

Without looking around much, he got an offer from a Brahmin boy from Hoogly District and fixed a marriage date without letting anyone know about it. And one day Pramila got married. Pradip heard the news and was bewildered that Pramila, who had accepted him in her heart as her husband, had changed her mind so fast and had married someone else. This was a great shock to him, and he could not tolerate the pain. He said to himself that if he stayed in Bengal he would never be able to forget her. So one night he disappeared from his house and no one saw him again.

Meanwhile Sanjaya, who had been kidnapped by the magician, was adapting well to a new kind of life. He had been brought into a community of magicians, who also sold herbs and medicines for gout, piles and snake bites. By using mantras they were also able to cure people possessed by ghosts. Some older magicians would draw blood by sucking through a bull's horn to cure gout, arthritis and other nerve and muscle pain. Sanjaya learned all those healing things, but he was more interested in the magic done by sleight of hand. He began to learn magic tricks by working with the magician, and he became so expert that sometimes even the professional magicians could be tricked by him.

The magician had great hope for Sanjaya, but he was afraid that if he took him to the cities he would be recognized as one who didn't belong to a tribe of magicians. Sanjaya was of fair complexion, tall and handsome, with a muscular body, whereas other people of the community were dark, ugly, thin and short.

The magician used some oil on Sanjaya's skin, which made him darker. From working in the sun without clothes, working in the dirt and eating very poor food, his whole appearance began to change. Gradually the magician started taking him to small towns. Sometimes Sanjaya would show the magic tricks and his master would work as his assistant. Whenever Sanjaya worked as the magician he would collect more money than when his master worked. His expertise in sleight of hand, his artful way of talking and his youthful, handsome body attracted crowds who donated money generously.

The magician was an opium addict. He would spend much money buying opium. Opium was his life. Without opium he had no strength to walk, talk or show magic. So most of the time he would tell Sanjaya to do the show alone, and he'd leave for the market to buy more opium. Sanjaya was a young boy, but soon he began to handle the magic show without his master's help.

Sanjaya almost forgot who he was, where his home was,

and who were his parents, brothers and sister. He began to identify with himself as a magician who traveled to different towns and cities to make money.

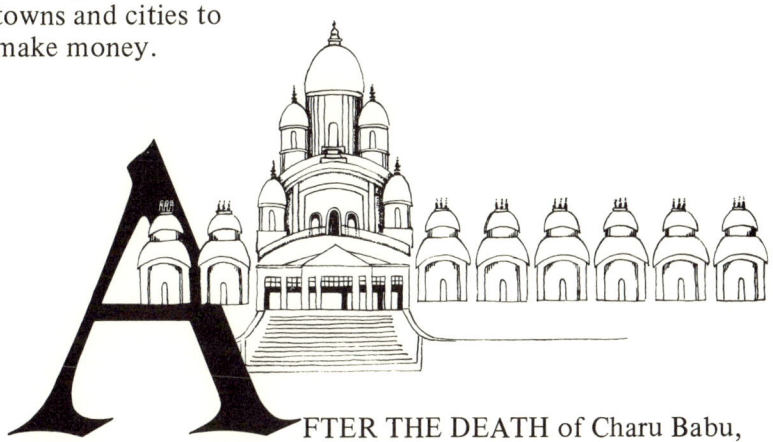

AFTER THE DEATH of Charu Babu, Vijaya, the poet, left his home and for some time he stayed in Dakshineshwara Temple, on the River Ganga outside of Calcutta. There he would chant spiritual songs with devotees and sometimes he would read aloud his poem on Ramakrishna Paramahamsa. Some time passed like this, and one day Vijaya heard sannyasins talking about a religious festival to be held in Allahabad during the winter; spiritual people from all of India would collect there. Vijaya thought it a good idea to go to Allahabad and attend the festival so that he could write poems about it. Although there was still a month before the start of the festival, Vijaya left for Allahabad.

He went straight to Triveni, a junction of three rivers—Ganga, Yamuna and Saraswati. He began to live in a temple at night, and during the day he would sit by the bank of River Ganga and write poems. Now Vijaya's appearance was completely like that of a renunciate. He had long hair, beard and moustache, and he wore only one cloth tied around his waist and hanging to the knees, with nothing on his upper body. He would carry a bag with his notebook on his shoulder—he had no other possessions. So everyone thought he was a monk and would feed him good food. Sometimes people would give him money too, when they realized he was an educated man and a poet.

The festival started in Allahabad, and Triveni was filled with people. The banks of the rivers Ganga and Yamuna, which had been empty a few days before, turned into a big city of spiritual people—hermits, monks and pilgrims. Vijaya was very happy to see this new city, and he would visit saints in their tents. He wrote poems on the glory of saints and read them to the pilgrims.

Sometimes he sat all alone in a secluded place by the bank of the River Ganga and watched the peaceful flow of the water. He would sit for hours by the river, his mind completely dissolved in his poems. One day, while Vijaya was all alone looking at the river, a man came to the same place and jumped in the river. He submerged himself one hundred and eight times while chanting certain mantras; and then he offered water to the sun by taking it in his palms one hundred and eight times, again chanting mantras. He came out of the water and his whole body was very cold and trembling. He thought he should lie down somewhere on the sand to get warm in the sun. He went forward and saw a renunciate sitting on the sand. The man bowed to Vijaya and said, "Swamiji, can I sit here?" Vijaya nodded his head and the man sat down at Vijaya's feet, turning his back towards the sun.

After fifteen or twenty minutes the man was warm and said, "Sir, from which place do you come? Do you see, everywhere there are people? People from all over India are here." The man didn't wait to listen to Vijaya's answer. He again said, "I heard that a great saint of the Himalayas, whose name no one knows, but people call him Mahavatar Babaji, comes to take a bath in the holy River Ganga during this festival. Some people see him and some don't. I am from Allahabad and I have tried to see him for several years, looking around among saints and secluded places, but I've never found him. I know he lives in a cave on Dronagiri Mountain in Almora district. The name of the place is Pandukholi. It is said that five brothers, Pandavas of the Mahabharata battle,* came to

---

* The Mahabharata is an Indian epic from about the sixth century B.C. which symbolizes the struggle between the forces of good and evil.

this place once and stayed in the same cave. It is also said that Mahavatar Babaji was in the battle of Mahabharata. His name was Kripacharya, one of the seven immortals."

Vijaya had heard a little about Mahavatar Babaji, so he listened to the talk of this man very keenly. He began to think, "This man has given me complete information about the cave. Perhaps it's a message from God for me to go there. That is probably the reason I came to Allahabad. I heard Babaji Maharaj showers his grace in miraculous ways."

The man again started speaking: "You can go to Kathgodam by train and from there by bus to Ranikhet. From Ranikhet you have to go by foot. Dwarahat is a little town on the way; from there climb up to Dronagiri." While he was talking Vijaya closed his eyes and started visualizing the whole journey. When the man saw the sannyasin sitting with his eyes closed he stopped talking. He closed his eyes in the same way and began to meditate.

Vijaya silently stood up and walked away. After a while the man opened his eyes and found that the sannyasin had disappeared. He was very surprised and began to look around, but he could not see him anywhere. He began to think, "Maybe that was Mahavatar Babaji Maharaj. He disappeared before my very eyes. No one else has such powers. He *is* Mahavatar Babaji." He ran yelling with much emotion, "Mahavatar Babaji Maharaj of Himalayas just visited! I could not recognize him, but when he disappeared before my very eyes like a fog disappears when the sun comes up, then I knew he really was Babaji Maharaj! All the time I was talking he remained silent with his eyes closed, and then all of a sudden he disappeared. I heard he is the only saint who can fly in the sky, walk on the water's surface, sit on fire and appear and disappear in a moment."

Those who heard him trusted him because he was so emotional and excited. They also started saying that Mahavatar Babaji was at the festival. Several people followed the man to look for Mahavatar Babaji. In the meantime Vijaya reached the train station and left for Kathgodam. From Kathgodam he traveled to Dronagiri Mountain and began to live there in a temple. He started visiting the cave every day but never dared to stay there. He had faith that some day he would find Mahavatar Babaji sitting inside the cave.

After marriage, Pramila went to her husband's house in Hoogly. She was angry and in much pain. She felt cheated, because she had not been informed of the date of marriage. She was not asked if she wanted to marry the man, and she had no time to tell Pradip. Her new husband was a shopkeeper and a very miserly man. He only wanted more money. He married Pramila because he had heard that she was in love with a non-Brahmin and that her brother was anxious to marry her to a man of her caste. He was confident that Sunil would give him money as a dowry if he married Pramila. But Sunil did not give any money except for the usual wedding jewelry and expenses of the marriage. The man became very angry at Pramila and began to abuse her. He took away all her jewelry and asked her to write to Sunil to pay twenty thousand rupees or he would leave her and defame her. Pramila was not afraid of anything. She heard that Pradip had disappeared, and for her, life no longer had meaning. So she told her husband that neither would she write to Sunil for money, nor would she live with him. That very night she too disappeared in the darkness. Her husband got the jewelry, so he was not the loser. He did not even bother to look for her. He wrote a letter to Sunil saying his sister had disappeared from the house—probably with her lover. The relationship was finished and no more letters were to be sent in the future.

The disappearance of Pramila gave Sunil much pain. He was all alone. He said to himself, "My father wanted me to marry so that there would be a queen in the house. But from the day I got married everything has gone wrong. First my brother Sanjaya disappeared, and then father and cook died, Vijaya left the house, and now my only sister Pramila has also disappeared. I am making money from the jute mill, but no one is left to enjoy this money. Yes, my wife and myself and my child will enjoy it. But the mill belongs to all three of us brothers. How can I take all the earnings for myself?" Sunil told his wife about Pramila's disappearance without expecting that she would show any compassion. But she began to cry and said, "Sunil, from the day I came to this house nothing good has happened. I am a bad omen for you. What can I do? I am an unlucky woman, I guess. I pray to God that the mill may not suffer some bad fate. If it happens then we will become beggars."

To please his wife Sunil said, "Oh, no. It's not your fate. All are born with their own fates. Don't blame yourself. Be happy. I love you, Swapna. You are my only support." Swapna was consoled and began to look at household work with more courage.

NEARLY FIVE YEARS had passed since Sanjaya went with the magician. The magician was fully confident that Sanjaya would not run away. Due to his opium addiction, he was not as good as Sanjaya in showing magic, so Sanjaya would act as the head magician most of the time. But as the magician had much experience in different towns and cities, he would plan the traveling and arrange places for putting on the show.

Once Sanjaya and the magician were in Banares. This was the first time the magician had brought Sanjaya to the eastern part of India, close to Bengal. They put up a show in the main street of the city. This time the magician was showing the magic and Sanjaya was his helper. After finishing the show, Sanjaya took a bowl around among the audience for donations. While he was collecting money he met a man from his family neighborhood. The man could not recognize Sanjaya, but Sanjaya recognized him. All memories of his past life revived. He began to think, "Why am I with this magician? I have my father, brothers and sister, and they are rich. If I go there, then I don't have to work. I can live in my house happily." But he was very afraid of the magician. He knew he was a cruel man, who would not let him go back to his house.

That night they camped outside of the town, which was a safe place. In the town there was always a problem with the police, who would suspect all magicians of being thieves, pickpockets, gamblers, etc., and if anything bad happened in the town, they would arrest all such people. The magician had had enough experience with the police in the past, so he always chose a secluded place outside the cities to camp at night. The magician took his opium as usual that night, ate some food and went to bed. But Sanjaya could not sleep—he was suddenly very homesick and began to think of running away from the magician. It was midnight and Sanjaya stood up. The magician was completely senseless. He took all the money from the magician's pocket, and also he took the opium from the magician's bag and put it in the tea kettle. He knew the magician drank tea as soon as he opened his eyes. He kept the kettle with water and tea close to him so that early in the morning he could boil it and drink it without standing up.

Sanjaya left in the darkness for the train station. He was afraid of the police who would check people at night, so he was very cautious and walked through footpaths of fields and groves. He reached the Banares railway station in the morning and got a train for Calcutta.

The magician woke up and yelled for Sanjaya: "It's morning. Get something to cook from the market." Hearing no answer, he murmured, "He will never wake up unless I kick him." He boiled the tea and drank it. Then he stood up to waken Sanjaya. But he was not there. At first he thought he had gone to the latrine, but then he checked the pockets of his coat. His money was not there. He checked his bag, and his opium was not there! He said, "That stupid lad has stolen my money and my opium. If I find him I'll punish him so hard that he will remember it for his whole life! After eating that opium, he can't reach very far. I'll find him lying unconscious on the ground." He laughed and said, "Inexperienced thief! You trapped yourself by eating that opium." He rushed out of his tent in search of Sanjaya. He walked a few yards and the opium started intoxicating him. He said, "Oh, my legs are freezing. Probably I took a big dose last night. I am still dizzy." He sat down on the ground and lost consciousness. It was a big dose of opium diluted in the water, so for two days the magician remained there in the same state. When he came to his senses he went back to his tent. He said, "I don't know where that boy lives in Calcutta. I never asked his home address. Looking for a boy in Calcutta is impossible. Calcutta is so big it is like an ocean of people. But if I wander in Calcutta, by chance I can meet him. I know he was from a Brahmin family so I just have to search out places where Brahmins live."

The magician had no money. So he decided that he would move to Calcutta slowly by doing shows in different towns and villages. Probably after six months he would reach there. Until then Sanjaya would forget about him.

Sanjaya had left home when he was eight years old, and now he was thirteen years old. His body was completely changed. He was very tall, and he had a little moustache. His complexion was dark and his voice was deep. There was no similarity between the eight-year-old Sanjaya and the thirteen-year-old Sanjaya. When he reached home no one recognized him. The neighbors said, "He is not Sanjaya. He is a cheat. Probably he knows Sanjaya disappeared and Charu Babu is dead. By posing as Sanjaya he wants to claim a share of the jute mill." In the house there was no one who could recognize him. The cook was dead and Vijaya and Pramila were gone. Sunil was at the mill and only Swapna and her two children were at home. She did not see much of Sanjaya before, so she could not recognize him at all.

The neighbors did not allow him to step in the house. They were very furious and threatened to give him to the police. Although he related everyone's name in the family, still no one believed him. Then Sanjaya said to Swapna, "One day I was flying a kite from the balcony and you got angry at me. You smashed my kite and threw my thread reel down in the drain. Do you remember?"

Swapna said loudly, "He is Sanjaya! No one knew this story except Sanjaya and myself. I believe he is Sanjaya. He has grown up so much in five years that we can't believe it. But I am certain he is Sanjaya." The neighbors believed Swapna and so they let him go into his house. Swapna was very lonely in the house, and she was worried that Sunil was heavily burdened by household and mill duties. Now with Sanjaya's arrival she thought that at least she would have some help in household chores. She said, "Sanjaya, you two brothers left your older brother alone. How can he do all the work of the mill? After all, the mill belongs to all three of you brothers equally, so you should help him either in the mill work or in household work. Your father died because of the shock of your disappearance. Vijaya left the house and who knows if he will ever come back. And even if he comes back he will not be able to help. He's very crazy. Your sister got married, but she also disappeared.

"Forget all that happened in the past. We suffered a lot and probably you also suffered. Now I am happy that you have returned. Some day you will get married and have children. This house will be filled with two families."

Sanjaya was shocked by all the bad news. He simply said, "Yes, I'll stay home. That's why I came back."

At night Sunil came home and found that Sanjaya had come back. He wanted to talk to him, but Sanjaya was exhausted and had gone to bed early. Sunil said to his wife, "Listen, now you both should compromise. I need Sanjaya. I love him. I don't care if Vijaya comes or not. He was never close to me and he never cared about the family. But Sanjaya is a loving boy. He can give me much help."

Swapna said, "We have already compromised. I also love him. When you see him you will not recognize him. He is taller than you and acts like a fully grown man. He doesn't talk much, but he is not shy."

Next morning Sunil woke up and went straight to Sanjaya's room. Sanjaya was sitting on his bed. Sunil could not recognize him even though he knew Sanjaya had come back. He began to have doubts about his true identity. Sanjaya guessed his feelings and said, "I am Sanjaya. I lived in various places in the sun and rains, outside in the dirt, so my color is darker. Also I am tall so no one can recognize me. You know I had a scar on my thigh when I got hurt by falling out of a tree and you took me to the hospital. See, this is the scar."

Sunil said, "Oh yes, you are Sanjaya. You are so changed.

I really could not recognize you." Sunil continued, "Sanjaya, probably your sister-in-law has told you all the news. So I don't need to repeat it. I love you, Sanjaya. I need you. I am all alone. I can't do everything by myself. You can either help me in the mill work or in the household work, or if you want to go to school I'll arrange everything. You are a young boy. You can still go to school."

Sanjaya said, "Right now I can't decide, but I'll stay at home and try to readjust myself. When I left home I was kidnapped by a magician and I lived with him for five years. I adopted the ways of his living and now I am in a different environment. I am afraid to be with people here—to go outside."

Sunil said, "All right. Do whatever you want. If there is anything you need to tell me, just speak up. Don't think of yourself as an outsider. You are the shareholder of one-third of the whole property."

Sanjaya began to live in the house, but he did not feel that he belonged—he always felt a separation. Also he had great fear of going outside of the house, so most of the time he would stay in his room, or walk on the balcony and watch people on the street. In this way six months passed. By living in the house, eating good food and doing no work he gained some weight and his complexion changed to its original color.

One day, while Sanjaya was watching from his balcony, he saw a snake charmer with a basket hanging on each end of a stick he was carrying across his shoulders. The snake charmer was the very magician who had kidnapped him. He noticed Sanjaya from a distance, but Sanjaya saw him only when he put the baskets down on the street right in front of his house. The magician opened one of the baskets and took out a poisonous cobra. He raised its head towards Sanjaya, and then he put it down and pressed its tail. Sanjaya was well acquainted with this trick: the cobra was trained to kill people. The snake entered the house. Sanjaya thought that he wouldn't survive if he stayed in the house. The snake could hide in any hole and attack secretly. He wouldn't be able to kill the snake when it was inside a hole. So he hung a rope on the back of the house, slid down it and ran away.

The magician waited for three or four hours. He played his flute, and several children and grownups collected. Then he showed magic tricks and collected money. When his show was finished everyone left and the cobra came back. The cobra was still angry so the magician guessed that he did not get Sanjaya. He said to himself, "Probably he ran away from the back door. Had he been in the house the cobra would not have returned without killing him." He collected his baskets and went away. He would check the house at night.

After a few days the magician, disguised as a sannyasin, went to Sanjaya's house in the evening. He met Sunil and asked if Sanjaya was at home. Sunil said, "Oh, he is a ruined boy! Once he ran away for five years, and then six months after he came back he disappeared again without saying anything to anyone. I have lost all my hopes. I can't trust him any more."

The sannyasin showed his sympathy and said, "I travel to different places and if I meet him I'll tell him to go home. If he comes back you should inform me by letter. I'll come and talk to him about staying home. But don't tell him about me or he will run away." The sannyasin gave an address to Sunil and left.

After leaving the house Sanjaya got on a train without a ticket. He wanted only to get out of Calcutta as soon as possible. The train's destination was Delhi, so Sanjaya arrived there and somehow managed to pass through the gate without paying for the ticket.

In Delhi he wandered around, sometimes working as a laborer and sometimes begging food. He did not like Delhi; he was afraid of the noise and the crowds. So one day he sat down in a bus with a group of pilgrims who were going to Haridwar.

In Haridwar he felt safe. There were less people and all those who were there were spiritual people. There were places to sleep on any temple porch or in the rooms built for the pilgrims. There was no trouble in getting food. So Sanjaya was happy there.

---

* In India tickets are collected at the end of a journey.

ONE NIGHT Sanjaya slept under a banyan tree on the porch of a temple situated by the bank of River Ganga in a secluded place. It was a cool place, so Sanjaya was fast asleep even in the morning when the sun was about to rise. A sannyasin came to take a bath in the river by that same temple. He saw someone still sleeping in the morning so he chanted *"Hari Om—Hari Om."*

Sanjaya at once awakened and sat up. The sannyasin saw a very handsome young boy with long curly hair and big black eyes. He went close to him and said, "From where did you come?"

Sanjaya was a very experienced boy and could talk perfect Hindi and a few other provincial languages. He said, "Delhi."

The sannyasin said, "Are you from Delhi?"

Sanjaya said, "Oh, no, I am from Banares and came to visit Haridwar. I stayed in Delhi for some time. But now I think I'll not go back to Banares. I like Haridwar. The secluded places, the temples, the holy River Ganga—I like those holy people."

When the sannyasin heard that the boy liked holy people, he pretended to be more serious and said, "Well, if you are a new person to this area, you can stay with me. I have a little place in a mango grove. If you want to be a holy man, then I can initiate you into sannyasa."

Sanjaya said, "Some day I want to be like you, but right now I just want a place to stay."

The sannyasin said, "Don't worry about a place. Stay with me. Let's go." He stood up and Sanjaya followed him. Sanjaya was all alone. He wanted some company. Also he had a deep fear of the magician, so he was afraid to live alone.

The sannyasin and Sanjaya began to live in a hut in the mango grove. The sannyasin bought bright silken robes of orange color for Sanjaya and said, "Young man, you are very handsome; if you wear these robes you will be even more handsome. People will be attracted to you and they will offer money. You should be serious in front of people so that they will think you are very holy. If anyone asks you about me, then say you are my disciple and recently came from the jungles after doing several years of austerities. But it's better if you keep silence when people ask questions. I'll reply for you. Also, remember that your name is now 'Bal Yogi Hamsa Dev'."*

The sannyasin would go out early in the morning and come back by evening. He advertised Bal Yogi Hamsa Dev, saying he was a saint with several powers. Often he would bring pilgrims with him to meet the young saint. Sometimes he would say that he had initiated him when he was a tiny baby. Sometimes he would say that his disciple had come back from doing austerities in the jungle after attaining all powers. He changed his story according to the people he would meet.

Everyone who saw this young saint was hypnotized by his beauty, his seriousness and his silence. Gradually his name began to spread all over, and more and more people started coming to see him.

One day when a huge crowd was sitting in the grove, Hamsa Dev came and sat on a dais in the lotus posture. His face was shining from the reflection of the bright, saffron-colored silken robes. The sannyasin in a loud voice said, "Gentlemen, I think I don't need to introduce Bal Yogi Hamsa Dev. He is sitting in front of you. If I point towards the sun and tell people, 'Look, that is the sun,' then it's a stupidity. The sun is seen by everyone. People feel its light and its warmth. Those who don't know the word 'sun' still feel the light and warmth of the sun. I can only say that Bal Yogi Hamsa Dev is my disciple and by his hard austerities, devotion and faith in his preceptor he attained a high stage of consciousness. He possesses several supernatural powers, but since all those powers are considered an obstacle in spiritual practices, Bal Yogi rarely shows them."

Someone from the crowd said, "Yes, we can see the sun. But our ears are hungry to listen to a few words from the mouth of Bal Yogi Hamsa Dev."

Hamsa Dev gently shook his body and said, "The aim of a

---

* Bal Yogi means a yogi from childhood.

spiritual aspirant is not to attain powers: these powers are like a servant to an enlightened being, but one who tries to attain powers becomes a servant of the powers. I don't usually show powers, but sometimes, to develop faith in people, I have to display them." He raised his hand up and said, "Look at my hand." A handful of raisins had appeared. Again he raised his hand. The raisins vanished and a bunch of flowers appeared. Then he opened his mouth and showed a smooth rock from the River Ganga. Then four or five rocks of different colors came out of his mouth. He then swallowed all the rocks and said, "They have their places inside the body."

The whole crowd was amazed. The most surprised of all was the sannyasin. He dropped himself on the ground and bowed several times.

People offered their precious things and money to Bal Yogi Hamsa Dev. When the crowd left, the sannyasin collected all the money, jewelry and fruits and took Hamsa Dev to his hut. He gave him a high seat and, bowing to his feet, said, "Sir, forgive me. I did not know you really possess supernatural powers. Forgive me for advertising you as my disciple. Sir, I want to serve you for the rest of my life."

Hamsa Dev did not say anything but maintained his holiness by being serious. Now the sannyasin began to serve him like a servant. Nevertheless, he was very alert in collecting the offerings. Hamsa Dev was now very popular all over Haridwar as an enlightened and powerful saint. He would sit in the grove from morning until night, and thousands of people would come to see him and offer money.

The sannyasin's fate began to shine like a sun. He was receiving much more respect than ever before. Within six months the mango grove changed into an ashram with a temple of Lord Shiva in the middle. Now Hamsa Dev began to wear jewelry, which made him appear even more splendid.

People often heard someone singing spiritual songs on the other side of the River Ganga. Sometimes they were in Hindi, and sometimes in Bengali. Hamsa Dev also heard the songs and asked, "Who is that singer?"

Someone said, "He is a crazy man. He wears dirty and torn clothes, his hair and beard are long and matted for lack of combing. Sometimes he runs and cries, and sometimes he sings. He wanders all over the dry rocks by the bank. He sleeps on those rocks and sometimes begs food. He is totally crazy. That's why he never comes to visit you."

Hamsa Dev said, "I have never heard anyone singing with such devotion. Probably he is crazy to find God." Hamsa Dev would enjoy the Bengali songs and was eager to see the man who sang. He must be from Bengal. So one night, while all were asleep, Hamsa Dev heard his song and went outside. For a while he listened to the singing and then decided to cross the river. There was not much water in the river at that place during summer so Hamsa Dev easily walked across it. He saw someone sitting on a rock and went closer. The man stopped singing when he found Hamsa Dev standing in front of him. He bent down on his knees and bowed to Hamsa Dev with much reverence. With folded hands and tears in his eyes he said in his poor Hindi language, "Sir, I know you are all-powerful. I wanted to see you, but I felt unworthy to step in your place. I am not even worthy to touch the dust of your feet, but Sir, you are so kind that you presented yourself in front of me. You knew my desire to touch your feet. I read in the scriptures that God appears in front of devotees when they cry to see him. You appeared in front of me only to bless me. Sir—you are God hiding in the form of this body. How can I serve you?" He bowed again to the feet of Hamsa Dev.

Hamsa Dev said, "You seem to be from Bengal. From which district did you come?"

The singer said, "Sir, I used to live in Baranagar, Calcutta, but now I belong to the whole world. I only want to be your servant."

Hamsa Dev said to himself, "Oh, he is from the block next to Ramchandra Mukharji Lane." He did not say that he was also from Bengal and the musician could not know from his manner of talking; there was no Bengali accent left in his Hindi. Hamsa Dev's sympathy naturally increased toward the man when he knew that they both were from the same place. But he maintained his prestige perfectly by not showing any kind of emotion.

Hamsa Dev very peacefully said, "Your devotion pulled me

here. You are a real lover of God. I came to see you by the order of God. I have already accepted you as my disciple. From now on your name will be Swami Naradananda. Forget the past—who you were and what you did. Identify yourself as a servant of God by the name of Naradananda. Go up in the mountains, visit the temples on the peaks, visit Badrinath Temple, and if God wishes we will meet again."

Naradananda bowed to Hamsa Dev's feet and, with tears in his eyes, said, "At last, by the grace of God, I found the path and I found my master." Without waiting for a moment he took off his rags and turned to leave. Hamsa Dev put his precious woolen, saffron-colored shawl on Naradananda's shoulders. Then the musician disappeared into the darkness.

Hamsa Dev went back to his room. He was very emotional and felt that he had not been behaving well. Naradananda's faith, devotion and dispassion had opened his eyes. He began to see that he was getting more and more trapped in money and false fame. He said to himself, "I was born in a rich family. If I had stayed there I could enjoy that wealth. A rich person can't eat more than his stomach digests—the same with a poor man. But discontentment makes both rich and poor miserable. Even if I am laden with gold and precious jewels, even if I become a king, still my desires would want more. There is no end to it." He could not sleep so he went outside, crossed the river and continued walking without any thought or aim.

Naradananda started visiting different temples in the mountains, and finally he reached Badrinath Temple, where he felt much peace. He would sit in the wilderness of the mountains and sing, his voice resounding in the chain of mountains.

When he reached Badrinath winter was about to start. During winters the doors of the temple are closed and no one lives there. Naradananda did not want to leave the place, but he had no means of staying. So he decided to go to other places, but Naradananda had no knowledge of sacred places in the Himalayas. Some other sannyasins were also planning to travel, so he asked them where to go. One of the sannyasins said, "Why don't you take a round? Go to Dwarahat and visit Pandukholi Cave on Dronagiri Mountain; it's a cave of Mahavatar Babaji Maharaj, who has kept the same body for more than

[183

five thousand years. But he appears and disappears. Those who are lucky can meet him. He appears to those who have extreme desire to see him."

Naradananda at once remembered how his master presented himself because of his desires. Now he wanted to meet this great saint. He said, "All right, I'll go to Pandukholi. Where will I go after Pandukholi?"

The sannyasin said, "You can go to Ranikhet. From there you can either go to Almora or you can go to Haridwar via Ramnagar."

Naradananda bowed to the temple before the doors closed for the whole winter and resumed his journey.

HAMSA DEV, after leaving his place, arrived in a dense jungle. It was a place where wild elephants roamed. No one dared to go into this jungle except thieves, who would hide in caves, or sometimes the villagers, who would collect grass for their animals. It was morning and Hamsa Dev was very tired. He sat down under a tree and fell asleep. A group of bandits passing through the jungle saw a young man, richly dressed and wearing jewelry. One of the bandits said, "Oh, when God gives food, it falls right in the mouth. Look! He is wearing jewelry and sleeping here like a king. Foolish boy! Maybe he stole it from somewhere." The thieves surrounded him and took off all his jewelry and robes. Hamsa Dev was not afraid of anything; he was not even sad at being robbed. The robbers said, "Young man, God saved your life. You did not resist. Otherwise, we would have killed you." And they all disappeared into the jungle.

Hamsa Dev remained sitting under the tree wearing nothing but a loincloth. After a while, when the sun was quite high, a group of villagers came to collect grass. They saw the young man and went up to him. One of them said, "Why are you sitting in this dangerous jungle? It is a place of elephants, snakes and other dangerous animals. It's a hideout of bandits. If they see you, they will suspect you are a spy and kill you."

Hamsa Dev said, "I am not afraid of elephants, snakes or other animals. I am not afraid of thieves. I am not afraid of death anymore. I want to go some place where I can find peace."

Another villager said, "You are a young man. Sometimes in youth a person gets momentary dispassion and leaves everything to become a renunciate, but then he develops pain when he can't retain dispassion. Why don't you go back to your home? Your parents might be crying for you. Young man, renouncing the world is for those who have enjoyed all worldly pleasures; then in their old age they seek peace. That's why they renounce the world."

Another villager said, "If you go straight along this footpath for four miles you will find a forest motor road. That road goes to Ramnagar town. But you have to walk ten miles to get there. From Ramnagar you can get a train for any place."

Hamsa Dev felt very uncomfortable around those people. He was a person who had been so highly respected a few days before, and now he was being considered a foolish runaway boy. His ego was hurt and he said, "Thank you, villagers, for your advice, but I don't have to go back to my home. My home is the whole world." He stood up and took the footpath. On the way Hamsa Dev thought that he had played a very bad game with that sannyasin in Haridwar. He had cheated himself. If he had not met Naradananda, probably he would still remain trapped in the marsh of money, name and fame. He had to find someone to guide him so that he would be able to attain peace. He walked all day long and that night he reached Ramnagar town.

In the darkness he could not find a place to stay. It was cold, so he went straight to the railway station and sat down in one corner of the passengers' waiting room. It was very crowded and noisy, but Hamsa Dev was tired and he fell asleep. In the morning he woke up and went to see the town. He had no money, but the stomach doesn't care if one has money or not. He became very hungry. He went to a temple with the hope that the priest would give him something to eat. But when the priest saw a young man standing outside, he yelled, "Are you not ashamed of begging food? You are young and strong. Can't you work and earn your livelihood? It's easy to become a beggar. We have no food for beggars." The priest came out of the temple and saw the shining face of Hamsa Dev. He said, "Oh, I am sorry. I thought a beggar was asking for food. I can see you are a renunciate. I'll bring food." He brought food enough for three people. Probably the priest was ashamed of his actions and wanted to show how generous he was by offering so much food. Hamsa Dev ate as much as he could, then he put the remaining food in an envelope made of leaves and left. He had enough food for the night so he was not worried about anything. He began to walk, amusing himself by watching people.

On the way, he heard some children yelling and clapping. He walked fast to find out what was happening and he saw they were teasing a crazy looking woman. Her skin was cracked from heat, cold and dirt. Her hair was tangled from not being combed. Her clothes were all rags. She was yelling in another language while the children were teasing her, so this made the children tease her more.

Hamsa Dev went closer and found that the woman was yelling in Bengali. He threatened the children and they all ran away. Using her language, Hamsa Dev asked the woman where she came from. The woman did not reply, but murmured, "I am hungry." Hamsa Dev gave her half of his food and again asked if she were going back to Bengal or if she had anyone here to take care of her. She again murmured, "I'll find him. I'll find him. I know he is not angry at me."

Hamsa Dev realized that the woman was totally crazy and it was useless to talk to her. She was not aware of anything— even of her body. So he stood up and left. He was looking for a place to stay outside of the town where he could be free. He walked to the riverside and found a hut. The hut was made for pilgrims to rest in or to change clothes in after bathing. There were several pilgrims taking a bath before visiting a temple of the Goddess Mother.

Hamsa Dev sat down on the bank, thinking he would stay in the hut at night when all the pilgrims would have gone. The pilgrims saw a monk sitting there and offered food and money. One rich man offered a woolen shawl so that the monk would be protected from the cold. Someone gave him cotton sheets. In a few hours Hamsa Dev saw that he was surrounded by cloth, money and fruits. A few pilgrims sat around him and one said, "Long ago a great saint used to stay here by the bank of this river. No one knows his name but everyone calls him by the name of Babaji Maharaj. He lived in Pandukholi Cave in the Dronagiri Mountains. He is an immortal saint and still sometimes appears among people. Several people have visited him in that cave."

Hamsa Dev said, "How do you get there?"

The pilgrims said, "That dirt road goes straight to Ranikhet. From there you have to go to Dwarahat. From Dwarahat you can go to Dronagiri in a few hours."

When everyone had left, he collected his new things and went over to the hut. It was now dark outside and inside the hut it was completely black. He crawled in, dragging his bundle. In the darkness his head touched someone, and then a voice started yelling in Bengali. He said, "Oh, the same woman is here." He took out fruits and said, "Are you hungry? Eat as much as you want." The woman said nothing, but she started eating.

When the woman finished eating she said, "Why did you come to this town?"

Hamsa Dev replied, "Oh, not for any particular purpose, but tomorrow I am going to Ranikhet. I don't know where God will take me."

It was late and they both went to sleep. In the morning when Hamsa Dev woke up, he found the crazy woman was still fast asleep. He put the woolen shawl over her to protect her from the cold and put all the money and remaining food close to her body. He took a cotton sheet to cover his body and left for Ranikhet.

The woman woke up and found the woolen shawl and other things. She was very surprised. She felt attached to the young man and thought that she should also go to Ranikhet to try to meet that kind man who had helped her so much. She collected everything into a bundle and hung it over her shoulder. She left for Ranikhet. It was very difficult for her to walk, because her feet were cracked due to the cold. On the dirt road sand or rocks would get inside the cracks and hurt very much, but she did not care about pain. She walked fast to catch the young man, but there was no trace of any man on the way.

Meanwhile, Hamsa Dev walked for four or five hours and reached a village. The children saw a monk sitting under a tree, so they informed the grownups, and they all collected around Hamsa Dev. Hamsa Dev was a very attractive person; moreover, all villagers had much respect and devotion for a monk. So they cleaned the place at once and made a good dais for Hamsa Dev to sit on. They made a fire to protect him from cold. They sang spiritual songs and offered food. When it was late at night the villagers saw someone coming towards them. At first they were frightened, thinking it a ghost, but then they thought that a ghost couldn't come so close to a monk, so it must be some crazy person. The figure, all covered by a woolen shawl, came closer and sat down by the side of the monk. The villagers saw a wild looking woman: she was very dirty, with blood coming out from the cracks of her feet, and legs swollen up to the knees. Her face was burned from the sun and the skin was peeling, which made her very ugly. The villagers thought that a crazy woman should not sit by the side of a monk. Someone said, "Don't sit there. Sit somewhere else. Don't you see any other tree here?"

Hamsa Dev recognized her and said to the villagers, "God is in every being. Don't see what she looks like, but see God dwelling in her heart. Her legs are swollen and her feet are cracked, but still her will is strong. She is a goddess. Don't hate her. Love her. Serve her and you will find God through her."

Most of the villagers were illiterate and they took the monk's words to heart and began to worship her. It was now late and all the villagers left for their homes. The monk and the crazy woman curled up in their places, turning their backs towards the fire to get the warmth, and fell asleep.

No one knew when the young monk left. Early in the morning when the villagers came to meet him, there was only that crazy woman sleeping. Hearing people talking, the woman also got up. She found the young monk had left. She also decided to leave and started collecting her things. The villagers saw that her condition was so bad that if she walked any more she would not survive. They told her to stay in the village for some time to get cured, but she could not understand their language. She said something that the villagers could not understand. But some women in the village picked up her bundle and took her to the village. They washed her hair, gave her a bath, washed her wounds and gave her a good place to stay. This was the first time the crazy woman had been treated kindly by villagers.

For two days she lived there, and the villagers served her as a goddess. By fomenting her feet with hot, salty water several times a day, her inflammation went away. They sealed the cracks on her feet with bee's wax, which cured the pain. They rubbed fresh butter on her face at night, and it healed the sunburn. They gave her new clothes to wear, which changed her whole personality. She began to bloom like a lotus flower. Although the villagers wanted her to stay longer, she clearly wanted to be on her way. The next town was Ranikhet but the villagers did not want her to walk for twenty-five to thirty miles, so they waited until a timber truck arrived, which was going to Ranikhet. The truck driver was a pious man and the villagers introduced him to the woman by saying she was a religious woman who wanted to go to Ranikhet. The driver happily agreed to take her, but there was no place to sit except above the logs. The villagers thought it was better to go to Ranikhet by sitting above the logs than to walk by foot. So they made a seat for her and the woman left.

Hamsa Dev walked for two days and then one evening he reached Ranikhet. He did not know where to stay there, and it was a very cold place—at night it was freezing cold. He had never lived in cold places before, so he asked people where he could find a place to stay for the night. The villagers told him of a place where pilgrims could stay for three days. Hamsa Dev went to the place before it got too dark. He went into the room and chose a corner to sit in. He had nothing except one cotton sheet, which he wrapped around his body. He squatted down, pressing his chest over his thighs and resting his arms over his knees.

The truck driver arrived in Ranikhet and stopped close to the pilgrims' waiting room. He told the woman by sign language that she could sleep there. The woman got down and the truck went on its way. In the darkness the woman entered the room and knocked against someone in the corner. Hamsa Dev was tired and was slumbering. He was frightened by someone's touch and jumped up shouting, "Who is it?"

His yell scared the woman and she yelled in Bengali, "Who are you?"

Hamsa Dev recognized her voice and said in Bengali, "Oh, you scared me. Sit here. It's very cold." The woman also recognized him and sat down very close.

Hamsa Dev began to think about how the woman was meeting him accidently again and again. There must be something between them. They both were from the same province—probably this was bringing them together, he thought. Then he said to himself, "It's more than that. I feel some closeness to her." He fell asleep thinking about this.

In the morning he woke up because he was shivering cold and could not sleep any longer. The woman was all wrapped up in the woolen shawl, so she was still asleep. Hamsa Dev at first thought to leave her without saying anything, but then he decided to tell her that he was going to Dwarahat village, and from there he would go to Dronagiri Mountain, so that the woman would not try to follow him or look for him. He woke her up and told her where he was going and that he had no aim or idea of where he would go from Dronagiri Mountain, or what he would do next.

The woman heard him talking, but she did not remove the shawl from her face because it was so cold. She did not say anything. Hamsa Dev thought she might be going somewhere else, or probably she wanted to stay in Ranikhet, or go back to Ramnagar, which was warmer and a good place to spend the cold season in. So he left.

When the sun rose high, the day warmed up and the woman

came out. Now she thought that her laziness had separated her from such a kind man, one who could be trusted and who belonged to her own province. She felt sad and lonely there. She collected her things and went into the town. Because of her language difficulty she only said, "Dwarahat" to people. They guessed she wanted to know how to get there, and they pointed out the way. It was a well-used road, with travelers on foot, bullock carts carrying goods and business people on horseback, so there was no danger of being robbed or killed on the way. The woman resumed her journey, but her feet were still not totally well and she could not walk fast. She walked slowly and cautiously, but after covering some miles her feet completely gave way. She could not walk any farther. The cracks on her feet had all opened up. She sat down by the side of the road thinking that she could neither go back to Ranikhet, nor on to Dwarahat; she was stuck in the middle. If she stayed there for two or three days to rest, then she would miss the young man. He would have gone somewhere else.

A mule driver, who was returning from Ranikhet with his empty mules, saw the woman sitting by the roadside in a miserable condition late in the evening. He took pity on her and thought that he could at least carry her to Dwarahat, where she could get help from other people. He asked the woman if she wanted to go to Dwarahat. The woman repeated "Dwarahat", and the man loaded her on a mule and carried her there. It was midnight when they got there and the mule driver had to go on to his village, so he took the woman from the mule's back and left her at an empty temple. The woman crawled to the temple and entered inside. Again by accident the woman knocked into Hamsa Dev, who was sleeping there. Hamsa Dev did not say anything, but the woman was frightened and said, "Who is it?"

Hamsa Dev recognized her voice and very peacefully said, "Oh, you reached here, too. Take a corner and sleep. I am too tired to talk. Probably you are more tired than I am."

In the morning they both woke up at the same time. For the first time Hamsa Dev could see her face clearly. He thought that he must have met her somewhere, in Calcutta or some other city, but he could not remember where. At Ramnagar when Hamsa Dev met her she was very ugly due to sunburn and dirt, but after the villagers took care of her, her skin recovered its natural glow. She was a very beautiful woman.

Hamsa Dev said to himself, "I don't know who she is, but she is someone with whom I am very closely tied. Meeting someone so many times is not an accident. Now I'll carry her with me, I'll take care of her, I'll serve her. I know she is crazy, she is sick and she is weak. No one wants her to come near them. But for me she is Goddess Mother. God wants me to take care of her."

The woman's feet were cracked and swollen, so Hamsa Dev decided to rest in Dwarahat until she got better. He went to houses to beg food. For Hamsa Dev it was very easy to get food. Everyone respected him as a monk and he was a handsome young man, so he always collected enough food for both of them. In this way they lived in the temple for six or seven days. The woman's feet were again cured and she was able to walk comfortably.

IN THOSE VERY DAYS Naradananda was living in Dronagiri Temple. He was all alone there, and in solitude he attained much peace. It was the first time he had really felt peace and he thought, "Probably it is by the grace of Babaji Maharaj, whose cave is not very far. Who knows? He may be sitting there now." He felt an extreme pull to visit the cave. So one day early in the morning he left to find the cave. He reached Pandukholi and looked all around. He found a cave, but he was afraid to disturb Babaji Maharaj if he were in there. So he said, *"Hari Om—Hari Om—Hari Om,"* from outside. Vijaya, who had been visiting the cave daily, was sitting inside. He peeked out and saw a young man wearing a saffron-colored shawl over his body. He was very handsome and Vijaya thought, "Babaji takes different forms—sometimes young, and sometimes old. No one else could be so shining!" He rushed out and grabbed Naradananda's feet and said, "Oh, Holy Sir, I knew that some day you would come. That's why I stayed in this cave for so long. Today you have fulfilled my desire. I heard from people that you come to bless those who have faith in you."

Naradananda himself was intoxicated in devotion. He could not understand what was happening. He entered the cave and sat down. Vijaya followed him and sat down, bowing to his feet again and again. Naradananda murmured to himself, "Those who have faith in God, God comes to them in any form," and he stood up. By chance his hands touched Vijaya's forehead and Vijaya felt as if electricity touched his spine. He sat up and his back stretched and straightened, his eyes were closed and he went into a deep trance. Naradananda came out from the cave singing in ecstasy. He climbed up on the mountain and sat down on a huge boulder. Sometimes he would sing, and sometimes he would go into deep trance.

That same day Hamsa Dev and the woman from Bengal also decided to go to Pandukholi Cave. They started very early in the morning because the woman could not walk very fast and Hamsa Dev did not like to leave her behind. When they came close to the cave, a mile or so away, they heard someone singing a melodious song. The song stirred the heart of the woman. She became very excited and her body got a new energy. She began to walk fast. Hamsa Dev's mind was concentrated on meeting Babaji. He was thinking that if he met him, he would ask him to give him a path to attain enlightenment. Sometimes he would think that if Babaji would just meet him, then he would not need any path. By his blessings he would attain everything.

They came closer and closer and Hamsa Dev was pulled to the cave, whereas the woman was pulled towards the song, and she started climbing up on the mountain.

Hamsa Dev entered the cave and saw someone with long hair and a beard sitting inside like a rock. He went closer and saw the man was shining like a star. He said to himself, "No one else can be so shining except Babaji Maharaj himself!" He dropped his body in front of Vijaya and prayed, "My Lord, I am a sinner, I am a cheat. But I never did anything consciously. You know all my present, past and future. What can I say in front of you? Holy Sir—save me! I want peace. I want reality. I want to get out of this darkness of ignorance. I am so lucky, Sir, that I found you here. I heard that you appear to those who look for you with faith." Hamsa Dev stretched out his hands and touched Vijaya's feet. No sooner had he touched his feet than an electrical energy passed into his body. He screamed so loudly it shook the cave. He sat up firmly like a rock and went deep into trance.

Naradananda was still sitting in his ecstasy when he heard the scream and decided to go back to the cave. While he was coming down he saw a woman climbing up. He thought that there must be lots of villagers around here and he would have to leave for some other place. But now he had to go down anyway. When he reached closer to the woman he yelled, "Pramila, you are here!"

At first Pramila could not recognize him due to his long hair and beard, which covered all his face, but when she recognized him she cried, "Pradip, it's you!" and fainted. Pradip grabbed her before she fell on the ground and brought her down to the cave, holding her in his arms. Inside the cave he put her in the corner and then saw someone else was also sitting there. He recognized his master, Hamsa Dev. He bowed to his feet with much devotion and as soon as his hands touched his feet he felt as if a strong electric current passed through his spine. With a jerk he sat up straight and went into a trance. All three men in the cave were out of the world. Pramila came to her senses after a few minutes and saw three men, all wearing beards and moustaches. All were sitting like rocks, and all were shining like stars. She could not understand how she came here. She saw the young man and she saw Pradip. Who was that third man? Probably the saint about whom the young man was talking on the way. He must be the great saint, Babaji Maharaj. She moved forward and bent to bow at the feet of the saint. As soon as she touched his feet her body began to shake and her spine became hot. It scared her and she moved back close to Pradip. Her body began to stiffen and she, too, went into deep trance.

No one knows for how long they remained in the cave in deep trance. But Pramila was the first one to come to her senses. It was because she had a great attachment to Pradip. Pradip also came to his senses, because in his mind there was always a thought of Pramila.

Pramila stretched her body and said, "Pradip, I have been searching for you from the day you disappeared. You might be thinking that I betrayed you. It was not my fault. My brother Sunil arranged my marriage without informing me of anything. It all happened without my knowledge. Fortunately, the man I married was no better than an animal, which helped me to leave him. Do you remember you once said, 'Even though we can't marry we can love and live in the hearts of each other?' This young monk who brought me here was sent by God. It was due to God's will I could meet you again."

Pradip said, "What I said was not true then, but it's true now. Real love is God. In God we all are one and will always remain one. It's only that the body envelops the reality. Pramila, open your eyes and see God and not the body." Pramila's ignorance of attachment washed away. She began to see love, God, reality—everywhere.

While they were talking, Vijaya came out of his trance and overheard Pramila's story. He guessed that the woman was his sister. For a moment his past memories revived and he said, "Sister Pramila, I am Vijaya, your brother. As soon as our father died I left home, and Sanjaya left even before me—that you know. I don't know who Pradip is. How do you know him?"

Pramila could not believe that the man whose feet she touched, which made her go into a trance, was her own long lost brother. She said, "Are you really Vijaya?" Vijaya's attachment, which had arisen for a moment, disappeared. He remained silent. Pramila went close to him and recognized him and said, "You are really Vijaya. Pradip was once my beloved and now he is the master of my spiritual life. You, too, were once my brother and now are my master. I found my brother and my master in the same place and both helped me to find the truth."

Now Sanjaya had also returned to his senses and he was listening to them talking. He was very surprised to see that the woman who had been with him for so long was his real sister and that Naradananda was her beloved. The man through whom he found the reality, the truth, was his own brother. "Has Babaji appeared inside all of us and opened our eyes through each other?" he wondered.

He said loudly, "I was Sanjaya once and now I am Hamsa Dev. Once we lived in the same place in Calcutta and now we live in the cave of Babaji Maharaj. It was Babaji Maharaj who has opened our eyes through each other by residing in our hearts. I have no desire to go back to the world. I have found that for which I was looking." He stood up and went out of the cave like an arrow, disappearing before Pramila and Vijaya could say anything.

Pramila said, "It was Sanjaya! He helped me so much. Due to him I could come here. How lucky I am that all three of you helped me and opened my eyes!"

All of a sudden a voice came from the cave, saying, "Pradip and Pramila, you have found the truth, but you still have karmas together to work out. Go back to Calcutta and lead a pious life there. Set an example for others that a householder can be a perfect yogi.

"Vijaya, you never liked a householder's life and you can live in Dronagiri Temple for the rest of your life. Sanjaya has broken all of his ties with the world and now he is no longer in the world."

Pradip and Pramila left for Calcutta and Vijaya lived in Dronagiri Temple, still waiting for Babaji Maharaj to appear in his physical form in the cave.

The text paper chosen
for this book is a 50 lb. Cream Antique
Sebago, while the cover is a
10 pt. Carolina printed in
five colors and tefcoated.
The body copy is set
in a cold-type equivalent of
The Times New Roman, a
highly-readable newsface
designed in the late 1940's by
Stanley Morison for *The London Times*.
The display heads and illuminated
capitals are set in Namaste, a
typeface designed especially
for this book.

Ashtanga Yoga Primer

Beautiful photographs illustrate this concise and easy-to-use manual of the eight-limbed Yoga. The contents include basic theory of Yoga metaphysics, beginning and intermediate practices of purification *(shat karma)*, breath control *(pranayama)*, meditation *(dhyana)*, mudras, and numerous postures *(asanas)*. The book also features a method of worship by light *(arati)*, as well as a unique series of hand gestures *(mudras)* to be used before and after meditation. Appended are schedules for daily practice, Yoga for pregnancy, suggested reading, and a glossary of Sanskrit terms.

Pages: *72*
Retail Price: *$4.95*
Format: *7 5/8 x 9, saddle-stitched*
Cover: *2 colors on Cambric Linen*
Illustrations: *93 photographs, 52 line drawings*
Publication Date: *October, 1981*
Library of Congress Catalog No.: *81-51052*
ISBN *0-918100-04-6*

A Child's Garden of Yoga

Pages: *108*
Retail Price: *$5.95*
Format: *8¼ x 7, perfectbound*
Cover: *printed 3 colors on 12 pt. Kromekote*
Illustrations: *172 photos*
Publication Date: *May, 1980*
Library of Congress Catalog No.: *80-80299*
ISBN *0-918100-02-X*

This sensitively-designed guidebook to Yoga really can be shared by children and adults. Ancient practices spring to life in 164 photographs of children demonstrating them as they are described in easy-to-follow directions. Children delight in seeing other children doing the postures, and they will invariably try them themselves. Postures for ages three to six are presented in one section, those for ages six to twelve in another, and a third section shows how to turn *asanas* into games and a lot of fun.

Also included are deep breathing exercises, a guided relaxation, and several meditations written especially for children. All of these practices can be a remarkably effective tool for channeling a child's high spirits and for strengthening both body and mind.

Hariakhan Baba ⦀ KNOWN, UNKNOWN

Hariakhan Baba has appeared recurrently for thousands of years throughout the Himalayan districts of northern India. Mentioned in Yogananda's *Autobiography of a Yogi* as "Mahavatar Babaji", he is one of India's most advanced yet little-known saints.

Baba Hari Dass, himself a lifelong yogi and native of the region Hariakhan Baba frequented, compiled this collection of stories from his own experience as well as from the first-hand accounts of many people whose lives Hariakhan Baba touched. A chapter of remarkable stories about other little-known Himalayan saints concludes this unique and inspiring book.

The photographs in this collection are the first ever published in the West.

Pages: *96*
Retail Price: *$2.50*
Format: *4¼ x 6½, perfectbound*
Illustrations: *18 photographs*
Publication Date: *February, 1975*
Library of Congress Catalog No.: *75-3838*
ISBN *0-918100-00-3*

Silence Speaks ||| FROM THE CHALKBOARD OF BABA HARI DASS

Pages: *224*
Retail Price: *$4.95*
Format: *5½ x 8½, perfectbound*
Cover: *Full color on 10 pt. Kromekote*
Illustrations: *52 ink drawings by Dharani Dass and photography by William B. Giles*
Publication Date: *January, 1977*
Library of Congress Catalog No.: *76-53902*
ISBN *0-918100-01-1*

A rounded handful of teachings from the chalkboard of Baba Hari Dass, *Silence Speaks* examines the topics of liberation, mind, life and death, relationships, desires, and Yoga. This volume of questions and answers was assembled from Babaji's philosophical writings, from letters to devotees, and from lively exchanges at weekly gatherings with people interested in the philosophy and practice of Yoga. In replies to seekers' questions that often express the pain and confusion of life, Baba Hari Dass compassionately affirms the power within each individual to attain peace.

Forthcoming Children's Books

CAT AND SPARROW

We know you will enjoy this delightful parable, written by a man who has mastered the art of teaching by playing. Here he tells the story of a devious cat who stalks a sparrow under the guise of friendship. The bird, however, is well-aware of the cat's true nature and soon outwits it. Uniquely illustrated by three-color woodblock prints.

MYSTIC MONKEY

More than just stories, the tales in *Mystic Monkey* are alive with fantasy, acts of courage and adventure, and offer a variety of provocative messages for young readers, 9–13. The beautifully rendered illustrations breathe life into a plethora of unusual characters and settings.

Order Form

Please send the following book(s) to:

Name_____

Address_____

City_____ State_____ Zip_____

No. Copies   Totals

_____ Ashtanga Yoga Primer . . . .@ $4.95 _____

_____ A Child's Garden of Yoga . . . .@ $5.95 _____

_____ Sweeper to Saint . . . .@ $6.95 _____

_____ Silence Speaks. . . . .@ $4.95 _____

_____ Hariakhan Baba: Known, Unknown. . . .@ $2.50 _____

Subtotal _____

California residents add 6% sales tax _____

Shipping ($1.00 for first book, $.50 each additional) _____

TOTAL ENCLOSED _____

Ordering Address:
Sri Rama Publishing
P.O. Box 2550
Santa Cruz, CA 95063